THE
HAPPINESS
RECIPE

THE HAPPINESS RECIPE

A Powerful Guide to
Living What Matters

REBECCA C. MORRISON

Published by Untangle Happiness

Edited and designed by Girl Friday Productions
www.girlfridayproductions.com

Design: Paul Barrett
Project management: Alexander Rigby

ISBN (hardcover): 978-1-7367730-0-0
ISBN (paperback): 978-1-7367730-1-7
ISBN (ebook): 978-1-7367730-2-4

*To Don, Hayley, and Grant, the most important
ingredients in my happiness recipe.*

CONTENTS

AUTHOR'S NOTE

I've given it some thought, and if I were in your shoes, I'd be wondering: *Why should I listen to what this person has to say about getting happier?* Here's my answer.

I am a lifelong learner. I've devoted countless hours to both the study and implementation of happiness—because I'm genuinely curious. By design, this book is not a report on the state of the academic discourse around being happy. I'm not here to tell you about the theory or structure, unless doing so gives you the framework you need to take action. If you are looking for data, charts, graphs, and studies, there's other great work out there that will tell you all about how happiness works and why certain approaches are more effective than others. The reason this book doesn't report those things is that this book is about taking action. This book is about getting the tools into your hands that can help you live a happier life *right now*.

Every single one of the tools in this book is something I've tried *and* something I've used with clients, friends, or family. And not just that—each one has had a meaningful and lasting impact on their happiness. This approach and these tools are too good not to share.

To support the work you are going to do here, head over to my website to download the companion action guide and some other goodies:

www.untanglehappiness.com/happinessrecipe

Here's the deal: it may have taken me forty-four years to figure it out, but I was put on this earth at this time to spread joy. And in my estimation, that requires doing more than just talking about how happiness works—it requires doing. It requires taking brave, bold action. And it requires helping others do the same.

If it helps, as you read this book you can imagine that you are sitting with friends who are all there because they want you to succeed—heck, you could even start a book club and make that vision a reality. And you can even imagine that I'm there—find me on Instagram at the.butterfly.society or LinkedIn (www.linkedin.com/in/beckymorrisonbfs)—to walk down this path of self-discovery and action with you so that you can get clear on your happiness recipe—exactly what you need to live the happiest life possible, starting today.

Let's get cooking.

INTRODUCTION

Hello, friend.

Thank you for joining me on this journey. I want to introduce myself. My name is Becky. I am a mom to a daughter and son who are—at the time of writing—sixteen and twelve, respectively. I am a wife—married for almost nineteen years—to an amazing person and basketball coach. I am also a daughter to two incomparable people who've both had meaningful and storied careers. I am a lawyer who has litigated and managed law firms. I am a leader of teams and people. And I am a coach who is passionate about helping people lead easier, happier, more productive, and fulfilled lives. Since you are here, you probably want to live that kind of life, too.

I also suspect you are here because right now life feels difficult or overwhelming and you wish it were easier. Perhaps you are working hard but aren't getting the results you want, or you simply aren't enjoying life. Maybe you know what you want to do or what you need to be happier, but you just can't seem to get there. Or maybe you are overwhelmed by the seemingly endless choices and decisions. Perhaps no easy solutions or clear forward path seem available. Sometimes, or even a lot of the time, you might think that no matter what you achieve, you won't be happy.

I'm also betting guilt is a big player in your life. Guilt when your personal goals sometimes take you away from people you care about. And guilt when prioritizing those goals keeps you from performing your best in other areas. Guilt when you say no. Guilt when you say yes. The constant tension can be exhausting.

Your mind may be cluttered with thoughts about how other people perceive you, your choices, and your actions. And what their behaviors and words *really* mean or how they *actually* feel about you. I'm guessing you shape your assumptions into facts and generate a whole narrative so powerful it governs your choices.

How do I know all this?

Because I was you. And sometimes I still am. *Oh my goodness, friend, I have been there, done that!* I earned the grades, degrees, competitive positions, and dollars. I had the partner, the kids, the stable high-paying job, and the house—everything that, on paper, should have been enough. Yet life wasn't as fun, easy, or fulfilling as I'd hoped. I spent countless hours trying to figure out what else I needed to be happy.

Look, you are smart, have tons of potential, and can do almost anything you put your mind to. But you wonder from time to time if it is enough—if *you* are enough.

You have goals, but you've been wondering if achieving those goals is really the path to that elusive happiness you seek. And, sometimes, when you fall on that path, you decide it's just too hard and you give up. Maybe you know you want something different or more but aren't sure how to make that happen.

Finally, I'd bet my savings this isn't your first rodeo. This isn't the first book you've hoped would give you the system, approach, or idea that finally helps you build the bridge from your actual life to the one you want. You may hope this is the "magic key" book that opens the door to your clear and easy path to personal happiness.

This book isn't magic. There is no single system, approach, or idea you are missing. You already have everything you need to live as you want to live—you just haven't figured out how to put the pieces of the puzzle together yet. School and society have failed to support you in making the necessary shifts in your thoughts, feelings, and behaviors to piece together a happy life.

That is where this book comes in. I hope this book empowers you with meaningful thought makeovers, needle-moving activities, and practical approaches for each season of life so that you can create the life you want to live—the easier, happier, priority-aligned life of your right-now dreams—and the life that builds toward your future dreams, too. This book was born from both my personal experiences and my experiences helping clients and friends untangle their lives. In the client examples I share, I've changed some details to protect the innocent, or in this case, the awesome.

This book is about how to be happier where you are today. It will help you make the shifts necessary to have more of what matters to you. If you are staring down the barrel of a big change or transformation, this book will help you navigate it. Conversely, if you aren't looking to make radical shifts in your current reality—no career revolution, no move across the country—this book will still help you navigate your way to a happier, easier, more priority-aligned *right now*.

This book will not provide a one-size-fits-all recipe for happiness, because your recipe is unique to you. Nobody else out there needs exactly what you need, in the proportions you need, to be fulfilled and happy. Thus, this book provides concepts and tools you can use to identify the ingredients that matter most to your happiness, take stock of which ones you already have and which you need to upgrade or acquire, and begin combining those ingredients—connecting your ideas to actions through feelings and beliefs. We'll look at common roadblocks that arise as you seek to change your behaviors and explore how to overcome them in easy and practical ways.

This book is not the end. It's the beginning. It is the cocoon to your butterfly. And what I hope you will take from its pages is the recipe for building your happiest life. Right now.

Chapter 1

THE HAPPINESS RECIPE

Some people have light bulb moments; I had a bathtub moment. It happened in late 2005. It was a day like most days—I was working as a litigation associate at a large national law firm, and I was in the heat of trial preparation. I was juggling work and being a mom to a toddler. A full eighteen months into parenthood, my husband and I had gotten pretty good (or so we thought) at the dance of managing busy careers and a toddler. On this particular day, I had a full schedule, including calls to prepare our expert witness stretching late into the evening hours. And on this particular day, something somewhere in the world required my husband to stay at work. We both agreed his counterterrorism efforts were important and primary (this was his career prior to basketball). Thus, I picked up my daughter from daycare and went home to handle both evening conference calls and parenting.

Sometime around eight p.m., I found myself kneeling on the floor of the bathroom, legal pad perched on the toilet seat cover, cordless phone clipped on the back of my pants, expert report spread out on the bathroom floor, and toddler happily splashing in the bath. I attempted to actively participate in a conference call with a team of legal experts *and* be somewhat present with my daughter at her day's end.

I was the person on the call responsible for taking notes— so while sudsing my daughter, I was muting and unmuting the phone and scribbling away on the toilet-top notebook. As I juggled pens, phones, and baby shampoo, I had a moment of clarity that brought two thoughts in quick succession. *Who says you can't do it all?* That was quickly followed by, *This is exhausting. This is unsustainable. Right now, I'm being neither a great lawyer nor a great mom. What if I can't really do it all? What if I don't want to?*

In that moment, I realized—perhaps for one of the first times since my almost-two-year-old daughter was born— that while I enjoyed being a lawyer, I also really loved being a mother. I suddenly awakened to the notion that I had more in my life—a daughter and a husband—and I finally began to ask myself what I really wanted. I was finally beginning to understand that my happiness depended on figuring out what really mattered to me—not what other people said should matter.

I've covered a lot of ground since that day in 2005, and based on my own life, my decades of people work, and my coaching work, I've figured out that the recipe for maximum happiness is pretty simple:

Do more of what matters most to you—and let go of the rest.

I call this priority-aligned living. Ultimately, identifying what you need or want, and then working to make sure your beliefs, feelings, and time (a.k.a. your energy) match that, is truly the recipe for living a happier, easier life.

Priority-aligned living is making a deliberate decision to spend your time, energy, and efforts on the things that matter most to you and being willing to let go of the rest—even when it is hard. Priority-aligned living does not seek perfection; it only provides a framework for decision-making, problem-solving, and time spending. Priority-aligned living reveals that what often holds us back is an unwillingness or inability to be honest with ourselves and others about what we really want or what really matters to us, and a failure to live in alignment with those things. Priority-aligned living is not an end state; it is honed with each decision we make. Priority-aligned living is flexible and highly individual—sometimes it requires you to make hard choices; but they are *your* choices. There are no wrong answers in priority-aligned living, only *your* answers. And if they are true to you, they can't be wrong.

I want to take a moment here to talk about balance. Balance is often misunderstood. Many people think that having balance means having an equal or balanced amount of each of the things in their life—enough fun to offset the work, for example. In priority-aligned living, balance isn't about evening out the things in your life, it is about matching your time, energy, and resources to your priorities. For example, if you are in a job-first season, balance isn't necessarily about introducing more social time—rather, it's about making sure that you are devoting time and energy to what matters most to you. As with all balancing acts, it's rarely possible to maintain your balance perfectly for any length of time. Now's a good time to get comfortable with the no-end nature of aligning your energy and priorities. There is no box to check or degree to receive. This balance is a skill to be practiced. And in many ways, that practice is required daily.

So if you are hoping you'll ride into the sunset with perfected and everlasting balance, it is probably a good time to dispel that notion. Let's drop the idea that you'll arrive at some glorious end state in which you achieve a perfect match between your priorities and energy and therefore achieve perpetual happiness. Instead, let's equip you with tools to more easily course correct, problem solve, and decision make— which, in my experience, makes life easier and happier.

To understand why priority-aligned living matters to me, you need to understand where I came from. I was raised by two exceptional—but very different—people. Both of my parents changed careers when I was in preschool. My father attended seminary and became a Lutheran pastor. My mother went to law school and became a lawyer, spending her entire post–law school career at a large multinational company. My mom was really good at her job (so was my dad, but that's not relevant to this particular story). As my mom rose up the ranks, she was given the opportunity to go through a leadership development program. In this program, she was required to get honest with herself, and then with her family, about her values and priorities. She tells the story of coming home one particular evening—loaded with some trepidation—to have a conversation with my dad and me about her priorities. During that evening's dinner conversation, she told us that, for her, work came first—before family. It was her top priority. My preteen response was "Duh." She had been living her priorities without naming them for as long as I could remember.

When I tell this story, people often stop me here to provide sympathy, or to ask whether I was hurt by this statement. I'll be real with you. I wasn't hurt. While work may have been her top priority, I always knew I was important, and I always felt loved by my parents. And this wasn't about me. Learning that mom was claiming the priorities that she was already living felt like a huge relief. Instead of an implicit understanding, we now had an explicit understanding. We knew how things stood and how we would operate going forward. We knew what was important to her. And as a result, we knew how we could support her in achieving what mattered to her.

Respecting and accepting that work was first for my mom also impacted my dad's priorities. My dad willingly embraced her priorities and accepted the ways that they impacted his own personal and professional priorities. And because we loved her and cared about her happiness, we were glad to know how we could contribute to it. I think of this particular childhood moment often, but most especially when I am called to claim what matters. When I do, I am reminded that, while I might be hesitant to say what I really need for fear it might hurt someone's feelings, being honest and true is almost always a gift.

Just because priority-aligned living is simple doesn't mean making the shift to living that way is easy—if it were easy, everyone would be doing it. Instead, I've noticed that the roadblocks that get in the way of living happy and easy lives often come from one of three mismatches or gaps. I call these:

1. **The Authenticity Gap**
2. **The Emotional Energy Gap**
3. **The Physical Energy Gap**

As you move through the chapters of this book, you will evaluate and work to close these three potential gaps in your life. Let's take a closer look.

THE AUTHENTICITY GAP

The Authenticity Gap is created when we don't name and claim our priorities—either to ourselves or to others. It occurs when what we *say* we think, want, or need isn't *really* what we think, want, or need. This typically happens because (a) we are letting other people tell us what we should want, or (b) we think we can't have or don't deserve what we really want.

Your Authenticity Gap probably started at a young age. Think back to the first time you went along with what someone else wanted to do, even though it wasn't what you wanted to do, because you wanted acceptance, to fit in, or to keep the peace. Don't get me wrong—sometimes acceptance, fitting in, or keeping the peace is more important than doing what you want. And perhaps these were useful strategies when you were younger and more dependent on others to get your needs met.

As an adult, you are fully capable of meeting your own needs; yet you may still use these outdated strategies. Unfortunately, they no longer serve the purposes they once did. Now you might notice that when you prioritize acceptance, fitting in, and peacekeeping over the things that actually matter to you, you feel resentful. This unhappiness can be traced directly to your Authenticity Gap. The resentment comes from not being honest with yourself and others about what matters to you.

Your Authenticity Gap also grows when you set goals around what you think you should do but really don't want to do. For example, you went to graduate school because you were supposed to or because it was the logical next step, but now you aren't feeling happy or fulfilled in your professional career—that is an Authenticity Gap. Or maybe when you knew it was time for a job change, you only considered jobs that were similar to the ones you already had or were in a similar industry because that seemed like it made sense.

Both in the exercises throughout this book *and* in your life beyond it, I invite you to be more honest with yourself and others about what you are really thinking and feeling, and what you want and need. If this seems too big or too hard, start by being honest with yourself. You don't ever have to share this work with anyone—unless you choose to. So be brutally, vulnerably open. That is how you will start to close the Authenticity Gap.

THE EMOTIONAL ENERGY GAP

We often forget to build a bridge across our Emotional Energy Gap. Once we are clear on what we want, we like to jump right from desire to action. The Emotional Energy Gap is tied to how we feel about ourselves and our ability to achieve what matters most. When our self-beliefs and our zone of emotional comfort/familiarity are incompatible with what we want, then lasting change is almost impossible. In personal growth, people often make strides on the Authenticity Gap—they can better identify what they want and need. Then they turn their energy to action. They focus on achieving that thing. Yet, after making progress, they slide right back to where they were before. That is because those old feelings and perceptions remain.

How many people lose weight and gain it back? Or pay off a pile of debt only to have it return? Or get so close to that final achievement only to decide at the last minute that it's not for them? That's the Emotional Energy Gap. It comes from a failure to recognize that our old beliefs and feelings create patterns in our lives. Without addressing them, it's hard to break those patterns and achieve new things. I like to think of this gap as your *why* and your *why not*. In personal development you are often asked to define your *why*—to claim what motivates you to make the desired change. This is a powerful step. Understanding why change is important to you can be a continuous source of motivation, something you can call on when you feel your resolve start to flag. But you also need to consider your *why not*. You need to understand the patterns and beliefs that will pop up to stop your progress. And where possible, you need to shift them. This book will help you work with your beliefs and feelings as you move from idea to action. It will also help you out of ruts and past the allure of old patterns as you take the necessary steps to achieve what you want.

THE PHYSICAL ENERGY GAP

Our happiness is directly proportional to our ability to spend our time, resources, and energy—our capacity—on the things that matter most to us. The Physical Energy Gap arises when the way we spend our time doesn't match our priorities because we either fail to articulate the order of our priorities or we don't make choices that are aligned with them. For example, if you were to say that your top priority (or goal) was "to be the best at work *and* at home," you'd be setting yourself up to experience the Physical Energy Gap. Inevitably, a moment will come when you must choose between work and home. If you choose work, you will not be doing everything you want to be doing at home, and if you choose home, something will have to give at work. If your top priority has a duality like this, you've failed to actually name a top priority. You haven't identified the *single* most important thing. You've identified two important things, and you might find yourself struggling to choose between them. It is one thing to get honest with yourself about what matters to you—closing the Authenticity Gap—it is a whole other exercise to put those things in priority order and then live accordingly.

Similarly, if your top priority is to be the "best at work," but you are pulled away from work regularly to tend the home front, you are also falling victim to the Physical Energy Gap.

You aren't aligning your energy with your priorities, and you probably aren't happy about it. You might think I'm saying you have to choose between work or home—you don't. Priorities can be a little bit more flexible than that. And remember, your happiness recipe is all your own. More on this in a little bit. Don't get discouraged if this is a source of tension for you. For now, understand that to close the Physical Energy Gap, you must define what matters most to you and then, as much as possible, spend your time and energy in alignment with those things.

To close all three of these gaps, you will need to be willing to choose more of what matters to you and let go of the rest. If you are not used to choosing what matters most to you— and frankly even if you are—you may experience discomfort as you do it more. One of the quickest, almost-immediate ways to reduce discomfort is to stop fighting it and expect it.

Weeks ago, after a particularly frustrating day, I found myself on a long, rainy walk in the woods. I'm not the out-doorsy sort, so willingly engaging with the rain was unusual for me. As I hopscotched around mud puddles on the dirt trail, I grew increasingly frustrated. The harder I tried to avoid the messiness, the more I bristled at the mess that got on me. Real talk: it is nearly impossible to walk through *a* mud puddle without getting muddy and wet—let alone *four miles* of mud puddles. At some point, I encountered a father and young son mountain biking through the trails. As they approached, the son whooped with joy: "Whoa, Dad, that last puddle, you got muddy water all over my face! So awesome!" And then it clicked. I could choose to fight the discomfort every step of the way, or I could choose to accept it. To go expert, I could even celebrate the discomfort like that young boy. Suddenly my frustration-fueled stomp through the woods became a rainy, muddy adventure—and, just as suddenly, the discomfort of getting messy became a lot less uncomfortable. The rain didn't stop. I still arrived wet and muddy at home. But by accepting the reality of the situation, I was able to enjoy, rather than struggle through, my four-mile hike.

ACTION STEP:
ANTICIPATE DISCOMFORT

Because I know making the shift to more priority-aligned living—like any change—might bring discomfort, I invite you to start anticipating it in the hopes that this awareness and expectation will mitigate it.

To begin this process, I encourage you to journal on the following prompts. Your journaling can take the form that works best for you: you can type, handwrite (in a notebook, on a paper scrap, as you please), record a voice memo, or talk with a friend. If you talk it through instead of writing, I do encourage you to find some way to memorialize what you learn (even if only to jot a few things in your cellphone notes app) so you can reflect back on it.

Really being honest about what matters to me is scary because . . .

Choosing to prioritize what matters to me might be difficult because . . .

Saying no makes me uncomfortable because . . .

Doing less might be hard because . . .

In addition to preparing for potential discomfort, this exercise may help you unearth some roadblocks you'll have to work through as you make this shift in your life.

Now that you've met the three major gaps that might be between you and living a priority-aligned life, we'll dive deeper into each in the chapters that follow. The rest of this book is split into three parts.

Part I invites you to close your Authenticity Gap by getting honest and clear about what really matters to you—about what you really need to be happier right now.

Part II guides you in healing your Emotional Energy Gap by building the foundational beliefs and feelings needed to support the action you will take to architect a happier life.

Part III provides the tools you need to bring balance to your Physical Energy Gap by actively matching your behavior to your priorities.

You'll walk away from this book with a clear picture of what matters to you and a plan for getting there. While this book is not specifically designed to help you find your purpose, the provided exercises may help you get closer to discovering it. That is what happened to me. But I also did lots of other learning and work—which I discuss in upcoming chapters. Let's get started.

PART I

THE AUTHENTICITY GAP

I want to be honest—remember that bathtub moment I described earlier? While I can still picture it vividly and regard it as a critical turning point in my thinking, I didn't respond to the call to do more of what matters and less of the rest right away. In fact, it took almost dying to wake me up to my need to take a serious look at my own happiness recipe.

In December 2005, I had an ectopic pregnancy and nearly died. A few days after Christmas, I was scheduled for laparoscopic surgery to remove a fertilized egg that had found a home not in my uterus but in my fallopian tube. Before I could get to the OR, the tube ruptured, resulting in substantial blood loss that threatened my life. Thanks to the good care of doctors and blood from donors, I didn't die.

Though I didn't realize it at the time, this was my real wake-up call. A few days after surgery, which included multiple blood transfusions, I returned to my litigation associate job at a large law firm in Washington, DC. That's right. I returned to work well before my body was healed and certainly months before my spirit and mind caught up. I went back to work because, as I saw it, that's what litigators do: they litigate. They work long hours, they show up for their clients before their loved ones and themselves, and they work. The more they work, the more money they make. And, at some point, they make partner and become rich and happy. So that's what I did: I put work before my health and family, including my daughter, because I thought if I made work my top priority, I'd be rewarded with opportunity and financial abundance. And, frankly, I thought it was what I was supposed to do.

A few months after my return to the office, the time came for my annual performance evaluation. At this firm, like many others, associates were measured on various performance factors. The one objective factor was the number of billable hours worked each year. To be eligible for a bonus, an associate had to have billed at least 1,950 hours. That translates to 7.5 billable hours a day every weekday for a year (with no holidays or vacations). To achieve a 7.5-billable-hour day, it is not uncommon to be at work upwards of 10 hours a day. In 2005, while raising a two-year-old, I had billed somewhere in the ballpark of 2,200 hours—or close to two *extra* months of 7.5-billable-hour days. I don't say this to brag but to objectively show that I was working a lot. My husband had a high-pressure, high-demand career in the intelligence community. Our daughter was at daycare for 11 hours a day during the week, and we took turns caring for her on the weekends. She was happy, healthy, and awesome. And though I never said it out loud, I enjoyed being a mom more than I enjoyed being a lawyer. Yet the mostly unspoken reality continued to be that I was being a lawyer a lot more than I was being a mom.

During my evaluation, I was told "off the record" by a male partner in the firm's home office, whom I had never met and never done any work for, that I should consider a different child-care arrangement so I could be "more present" at the office.

I lost my shit. There's no other way to say it. My honest-to-goodness first thought after he said this was: *Thank goodness that pregnancy didn't work out—if I can't do enough to make them happy with one kid, how would it have been with two?* I was so upset that I had to end the call. I think he knew he'd made a major misstep because, within minutes, the female partners in the Washington, DC, office (all two of them) were in my office to talk about how I could go part time if I needed more flexibility to balance my commitments at work and home. My response: "I billed over twenty-two hundred hours last year, why do I need to go part time?" Their reaction: stunned silence.

I was deeply unhappy. I was giving freely of my physical energy to an organization that clearly didn't recognize or value my contributions. I wasn't even sure I wanted to be a litigator, let alone a litigation partner, but I also wasn't sure I could give up being a lawyer after investing so much time, money, and energy into law school. I wasn't being honest with myself or the people in my life that I liked being a mom more than being a lawyer. I believed that because I had gone to law school and been hired by a good firm, I had to continue to charge toward law firm partnership. But, at the end of the day, I was devoting all my time and energy to an organization that wasn't giving me value in return. Basically, I was suffering from big gaps in authenticity, emotional energy, and physical energy.

To resolve these gaps, I had to first take the plunge and get honest about what really mattered to my happiness. I needed to close the Authenticity Gap. The Authenticity Gap arises when we aren't clear on or honest about what actually matters to us. Almost everyone struggles with the Authenticity Gap at some point in their lives. This is not surprising, because from the very beginning of our lives, we are barraged by messages from family, community, and the media telling us what we need in order to be happy and successful. These messages are so loud and pervasive that often—without our even realizing it—they become *our* messages. Closing the Authenticity Gap requires exploring which of these messages are ours and which are not.

Part I of this book guides you to close your Authenticity Gap. You will start by getting honest about your current reality and clear on what season you're in and all that brings with it. Often shifts happen in our lives—like my shift to motherhood—and we don't appreciate how those shifts impact our happiness recipe. We don't recognize that our season has changed and that our priorities need to follow suit.

Next, before you can do more of what matters and less of the rest, you need to take stock of where you are actually spending your time and energy. With a clear picture of your life today, the fun can begin—you can dream about what a happier *right now* would look like and what changes you might need to make. You'll start by dreaming without limits, and then take practical steps to figure out what is attainable now and what might come later. You will leave part I with a clearer understanding of the ingredients necessary to make up your happier *right now*—you will authentically claim what matters most to your happiness, and you will be ready to do more of those things and begin to let go of the rest.

Chapter 2

SEASONS

"It is her butterfly season. You get to cheer her on and watch her make her mark on the world. She can't do that from the comfort of the cocoon. And, oh, what a gorgeous butterfly she will be!" That is what I told my friend—a fellow mother who was wrestling with the heartache and joy of sending her eldest off to college. As I reflected on our conversation later that day, I thought, *I don't want my butterfly season to have happened at age seventeen. I want it to be right now.* And then I realized it could be.

I realized that we aren't limited to a single butterfly season—when we first take flight. Instead, we can have many beautiful butterfly seasons of varying size and scope throughout the course of our lives. And not every season of our lives is a butterfly season—those seasons that are marked by growth, transformation, evolution, and flight that is sometimes grand and sometimes quietly graceful. Some seasons are caterpillar seasons that are quieter, calmer, and full of consistent movement.

Other seasons are cocoon seasons marked by preparation, restoration, and resetting.

Life is a series of seasons—and sometimes the tension between how we are living and our happiness stems from failing to recognize the season we are in. Instead of aiming to be happy at some future point in life, we should aim to be as happy as possible in each season of our lives. And to be happy right now, we need to know what season we are in right now.

Consider the following example: Wearing a swimsuit outside in the winter in most climates would be a recipe for discomfort. You can't wish summer into being by putting on a swimsuit. If it's winter, it's winter. And if you do nothing more than wear winter clothes in winter instead of your swimsuit—in other words, aligning with the reality of your current season—you will be happier. You can take it a step further by finding ways to make winter more enjoyable, such as skiing and building snowmen. But even without doing more, simply accepting the reality of your season yields an automatic increase in comfort. This is because being honest about your season will help you begin to close the Authenticity Gap.

Now let's talk about the seasons of our lives. When talking about life's seasons, I don't just mean youth, middle age, and old age. I mean something much more specific and personal. To make this more concrete, I will tell you a little bit about three seasons in my life—the one that ended about two years ago, my current season, and the one I anticipate entering next.

I call the season that ran from about 2006 to 2018 my Working Motherhood Season. During this season, I had my second child, stopped litigating cases and practicing law, and came to terms with my choice to be a mother first. During this season, I started living a priority-aligned life. You might think I'd adopted the concept of priority-aligned living long ago—after all it's something my mom modeled to me during my adolescence. But the reality is that, although I had a front-row seat to my parents' priority-aligned lives, I didn't thoughtfully apply this concept to my own life until my Working Motherhood Season. Until that point, I'd been operating under the shadow of shoulds and wasn't focused on defining what actually mattered to me.

This season was born on the heels of a traumatic pregnancy loss and the disappointing evaluation conversation I described earlier. After that conversation, I realized it was time to look for another job. It had become abundantly clear that my current organization was not seeing the value of the effort I was giving. Within weeks, I was actively seeking my next opportunity. Initially, I thought the best solution would be to find a similar role at another firm with a better culture. I was working with a headhunter and had several preliminary conversations about potential litigation associate positions at other firms. Yet to simply switch firms, I would have to ignore the thoughts that had become louder since that bathtub moment. I couldn't stop wondering: *What really matters most to my happiness?*

I began to take stock of the things in my life—career, motherhood, marriage. As I did that, I really considered which ones made me happy. The more I considered it, the more I realized that continuing to work as a litigator in a traditional big law firm wasn't going to allow me to spend my capacity—time, energy, and resources—on what was most important to me. My top priority needed to be my family. I also realized that to honor my family as my top priority, I needed to shift my beliefs around success. I had made a substantial investment of time and money in getting a law degree. Many of my peers were still in traditional associate roles and headed for partnership. Externally-defined success would have involved staying the course and finding another litigation associate job on the partner track. My new, internally-defined success, on the other hand, pointed toward finding an interesting and challenging job in which I had more control over my schedule and hours so I could be more present for my daughter.

Ultimately, I realized that, in this season, parenthood was more important than everything else. Luckily, I found a position at another large DC litigation firm—with a twist. This position was an administrative position, rather than a litigation associate position. Because I was no longer bound to trial calendars and clients, I could have more control over my time and schedule. This was so valuable to me that I was willing to take both the title-prestige hit and a pay cut to make it happen. By choosing this particular firm, I was still able to work with some of the most talented litigators in the world. It was the best of both worlds in a professional sense. More than that, it allowed me to make my family my top priority.

Some of you might be reading this and wondering: *How can you say that during this season you were a mom first if you had a job outside the home?* This is what I meant earlier when I said priorities are flexible and individual. I'll explain more about my considerations. I have always known being a full-time mom wasn't the right choice for me. It's not just that our family needed both incomes—which was true at the time. For me to be a happy human and a good mom, I needed to do something that engaged my brain in ways that parenting didn't and gave me a personal purpose outside motherhood. When I say I was a mom first during this season, I am referring to the million small and sometimes large ways that I chose to put family over professional advancement. It meant taking leave time to be at sporting events, school concerts, and home with a sick kid— and not feeling bad, guilty, or that I was giving something up to do it. It meant saying no to the juicy project when someone else could do it, even if it meant less visibility for me and a missed professional opportunity. I was honest with myself and those around me—including my work—that when push came to shove, I was going to choose family over work.

To be honest, my Working Motherhood Season was not a perfectly executed dance of prioritizing family over work. This was not a decision I made once and then everything magically fell into place. Sometimes things would get out of whack, work would eat up too much of my energy and attention, and my happiness would start to decline. But by knowing where my priorities were and being honest with myself, I was able to make quick course corrections when these moments of imbalance arose. This season was also an evolution—it was a long season and, as such, it didn't look the same at the end as it had at the beginning.

Change happened gradually. As I practiced that balance of energy and priorities, I found myself more present for my family and less challenged intellectually. While an intellectual challenge was not my top priority, it had always been important to my happiness recipe. After a decade spent working in law firm administration, I was feeling a little bored. For me, boredom, like increasing unhappiness, is a cue that I am out of balance. Nothing was wrong with my job. I was working with great people who were doing interesting work. I was managing teams of people, which I truly enjoyed. But I was redesigning processes for the second or third time and solving the same sorts of problems over and over. I also realized that to feel more challenged in my current position, I would need to make work a higher priority, which I just wasn't willing to do.

I knew it was time for a change and that being a mom remained my top priority. As I looked for a new position, this knowledge drove the opportunities I would consider. I said no to a job with an even larger international law firm, which would have paid me significantly more but required more hours and considerably more travel. Finally, I settled on what might seem like a left turn to some. I left the legal industry entirely and took another pay cut to work for a small investment firm started by a law school friend. This job also required slightly more travel, but in exchange for that travel, I was able to work from home when not on the road.

Working from home meaningfully shifted my balance dance. Having even more flexibility and control of my schedule and gaining two to three hours a day by eliminating my commute were game changers. This job also deepened my appreciation for the entrepreneurial environment and greatly improved my understanding of wealth and abundance. Almost three years into this job, a confluence of events—particular economic conditions, my own growing boredom, and the changing geographic distribution of my colleagues—contributed to my decision to move on. Although I wasn't technically fired or laid off from this job, it sure felt that way. I found myself rather suddenly staring down the barrel of unemployment with no clearly articulated plan B. I began a frenzied process of applying for every job I thought I could possibly do. When you are a lawyer with litigation, management, writing, and technology experience, the list of what you *can* do is long.

Thankfully, during an early conversation about this shift, my boss, who was also a dear friend, encouraged me to really consider what I wanted to do next. This conversation marked the first time I admitted out loud that I wanted to be a coach. As I recall, through tears, I said something like, "I secretly want to be an executive coach." This was a scary admission. I was admitting that I wanted to explore a profession that had zero obvious connection with the years of schooling that I'd been through, the career I had built, and the vast investment of money and time they represented. I was also saying I wanted to have my own business and be solely responsible for my success or failure. Finally, I was saying that I believed I could help other people be better. All these enormous things in just eight small words.

This moment was, in so many ways, the birthplace of my current season. My current season is marked by several important characteristics: I am still a mom—but now to a high school junior and a seventh grader who need me to be present in totally different ways. I am still a wife—to the same man, but now instead of working in intelligence, he spends much of his time in a basketball gym, coaching and mentoring young men to be the best they can be, on and off the court. The big transformation in this season: I am my own boss. I am—for the first time ever—wholly in charge of how I spend my time and whether (and how much) I get paid. That is a big change for me, and it has meant a shift in my priorities. Because I am now nurturing a business, there are times I need to show up for my business or myself (so that I can show up for my business) *before* my family—a season-based shift in my priorities, which I'll explore further later.

The next season I am planning probably won't start for another five to six years. In that one, both my kids are off living their own lives, from under my roof or their own. That season will be one of the biggest changes of all. I may go from being a mom first to being a wife first, a coach first, or something else entirely. I haven't figured that out yet—and I don't need to figure it out to enjoy my current season's happiness. That said, I do think about it as I take action and plan in the current season.

Identifying the season that you are in is important for two reasons. First, accepting the reality of where you are helps you quickly identify behavior changes that can instantly increase the comfort of your current season—the equivalent of wearing a winter coat when it's cold outside. Second, as you move through the remaining exercises in this book, understanding your current season means that you understand the limitations on what you can seek to achieve or do right now. It's not an issue if you can't have every single thing you've ever dreamed about in the current season—our process helps you identify what you *can do* to begin to live a happier, more priority-aligned life today, while still planning for tomorrow.

ACTION STEP:
IDENTIFY YOUR SEASON

Before going any further, take a moment to define your current and next season. This exercise asks you simply to outline the season that you are in, and perhaps the next one you anticipate. This exercise is not asking you to think about whether or how you want this season to be different. I am not asking you to consider whether you are spending your time, energy, and resources how you want to. I am simply asking you to define your current reality. If you aren't comfortable with your current reality, this exercise might be hard or unpleasant That's normal. The purpose of this exercise is to become more comfortable in the season you are in—and that starts with being honest with yourself.

Here are some questions you can ask yourself as you consider this:

What do I currently spend my time on?

This list should include the broad categories of things in your world. For example, it might include family time, kids' activities, house care, job, networking, friendships, religion/spiritual practice, hobbies, wellness, or your partner. If you are having a hard time coming up with this list (which we will use again) you might want to look at your calendar or to-dos, as a starting point.

Who are the important people in my life right now?

In this question, the word *important* means taking up time, energy, or resources—your capacity. It doesn't mean who you *want* to take up your capacity, it means who *is* taking it? For example, your horrible boss may not be a meaningful and beloved presence, but he or she is important in this season because they are taking your capacity.

When/why will that change?

This question is designed to help you identify when this season might end. When the people, places, and things taking your time, energy, and resources start to shift, it's often a clue you are entering a different season. If there is no end in sight, or you aren't sure when the change is coming, that is not a problem. I promise this framework will enable you to more clearly see the change when it's happening.

Bonus Question: What is my winter coat?

Ultimately, your winter coat will probably take the form of acceptance, release, or adaptation. To identify *your* winter coat, you can consider the following questions.

If I get really honest about my season, what can I accept about it that immediately increases my comfort?

For example, if you are deep in the jungles of working parenthood, you may not have as much room for social activities—and it's okay to let them go (for now).

*Is there something that I can let go of or take on that
will automatically make me happier?*

For example, if you really hate cleaning, can you hire a professional cleaner?

*Finally, is there something I am trying to do that isn't a
match for this season?*

Instead of trying to force it, can you adapt it to be a better
match by meeting the underlying need in a different way?
For example, if you can't travel because the world is locked
down, what could meet the same need for adventure or
new experiences?

If a winter coat doesn't jump out at you right away,
don't worry. As you work through the rest of the chapters
in this book, your winter coat will, more likely than not,
become clear.

Based on your answers above, you can now formu-
late a one-to-three-sentence description of your current
season and the next season you anticipate. Here are some
examples:

*Example 1: I am pregnant with my first child. The current
season is my pregnancy, and the next season is the
early years of motherhood.*

*Example 2: I plan to retire in three years. The current
season is the last three years of my preretirement
career, and the next season is the early years of my
retirement.*

Example 3: I want a new job. The current season is one of job searching. What I do in this short season will radically impact what I do in the next season, which will start when my new job starts.

Example 4: I am living the same life I've been living for a while, and there's no end in sight. The what and the who are fairly constant. (If this is you, just pick a name for your season that makes sense to you.)

Remember, there are no wrong answers here. Your season really is *your* season—and however you define it is acceptable. Once you have your description, hold on to it. You will be referring to it in later action steps.

Understanding that life is a series of seasons allows you to focus on achieving a happier and easier life right now. Happiness isn't about working super hard today and taking a short-term hit so you can be happier at some hypothetical future point. Rather, it's about understanding the contours of what you want and need to be happy given the circumstances of your current season—and what you want to be building toward in the future. Then it is about doing what will increase your happiness in the near term.

Last thought—for now—on seasons. You may be wondering—is approaching life, happiness, and problem-solving on a season-by-season basis really just code for living a life more grounded in the present? The answer is yes and no. Appreciating seasons or chapters in your life doesn't mean you forgo planning for the future. Think of it this way, in the winter you prepare the soil that will house the spring seeds that will produce the summer plants that will become the fall harvest.

You can live inside this season in a way that prepares you well for your next. That said, being more present—ultimately being more grounded in the reality of today and looking for ways to appreciate and enjoy it—can only benefit you. Why wouldn't you want to be happier in the present?

Chapter 3

TAKING STOCK

Now that you understand the basics of priority-aligned living, you can start applying them to your life. In the next three chapters, you will do two things: take stock of where you are in your current season and map out where you want to go in both this season and the next. These two steps are critical to closing the Authenticity Gap. This is where you get honest with yourself about the reality of this season and what you need to be happy. I have witnessed, both with clients and in my own life, that it can be a struggle to do both of these things—and that's okay. We are going to start with the easier of the two. This chapter asks you to get honest—but not modest—about where you are today.

I'd like you to think of both taking stock and mapping using the analogy of assembling a puzzle. The analogy has natural appeal to me. My family loves a good puzzle. When we are together on vacation or during the holidays, there is usually a puzzle going. There is something soothing about the sorting, cataloging, and connecting needed to complete a complicated puzzle. It should not surprise you that puzzle solving is one of my favorite parts of coaching—working with my clients to untangle, connect, and find solutions to seemingly complicated problems. Clients often come to me looking to answer big questions like:

What do I want to be when I grow up?

How can I move from idea to action?

I'm so overwhelmed. How can I make it better?

I want to take the next step in my career—how do I get there?

To answer these questions, we work together through a process that looks a lot like assembling a puzzle. We:

Take stock of the pieces.

Find the edges and group like pieces.

Connect.

When trying to answer big questions like these or the one driving this book ("How do I live a happier life right now?"), the same process applies. Yet this isn't how many people approach their biggest challenges. When emotions are high or things seem hard, we often grab a couple of pieces from the many that are floating in our lives and try to connect them or understand them in a vacuum. It's rare that the puzzle can be completed this way—and even if it can, it's certainly not an efficient or easy process.

In attempting to take stock of what goes into solving this puzzle, people often make two mistakes: they try to solve it all in their head, and they aren't completely honest about the pieces of their puzzle. These mistakes contribute to their Authenticity Gap—creating barriers between them and claiming what they want and need.

People ineffectually try to hold and assemble all the pieces of their puzzle in their heads. It is the rare individual who spends time getting all their thoughts about an emotional or challenging issue out of their head in an organized way so they can take inventory, spot patterns, and make connections. Moreover, this is hard to do on your own. *So hard.* Even if you are an avid journaler, if you aren't reviewing and compiling your thoughts regularly, you aren't capturing everything. Trying to hold everything in your head makes it virtually impossible to be clear on what you most want and need—the result is that you will always struggle with the Authenticity Gap and, ultimately, the Physical Energy Gap. You won't be sure on a minute-to-minute, week-to-week, or year-to-year basis what actually matters. Therefore, you won't be able to match your energy to those priorities. You will be inclined to address the loudest pieces of your puzzle—the ones that seem urgent or even emergent. And instead of spending time building toward what matters, your time will be consumed putting out fires.

With almost every client I coach through answering the big questions, we reach a point where we must explore it visually. It can be a list or a mind map or a bunch of Post-it notes, but it must be something tangible, visible, and physical through which the client can see all the thoughts they are having and recognize that (a) they have a lot to sort through or (b) they are saying the same thing a bunch of different ways. In addition, exploring the big questions visually makes it *much* easier to spot patterns, which is critical to making connections that facilitate growth and change. Often it is by making the ideas visible that the complex and confusing become simple and clear.

I had a client named Benjamin. Benjamin was looking for a new job. He articulated that he either wanted to find a similar position at a new organization or make a meaningful shift to a new career entirely. I asked a couple of questions to explore this dichotomy, and Benjamin's answers were all over the place. I did what I often do when I'm feeling a sense of stuck or overwhelm from a client, I broke out the Post-it notes. I asked Benjamin, "Without thinking about whether it's the same position or a totally different one, tell me what you want your next job to look like." As we talked, I just started writing words and phrases that he said on Post-it notes. Then I stuck the notes on the table in front of him. A funny thing happened: as he reviewed the Post-it notes to make sure I had accurately captured what he said, he started to unconsciously sort them into categories. Some notes contained specific job attributes—salary, location, and hours. Others contained his skills—problem-solving, organization, and research. Still others addressed his work environment—open minded, team atmosphere, and autonomy. When Benjamin finished his general thoughts about what he wanted the next job to look like, I asked him to study the picture in front of him for a few minutes. He did and then he said something like, "All this stuff fits with the position I currently have—I just don't like my organization anymore. I thought maybe I needed to change careers to find happiness. I don't. I just need a different environment. And I have a list of what I'm looking for right here." It was so simple, but until we got it in front of him, it wasn't visible—or clear—to him.

The action steps in the next two chapters will help you get all the pieces of the puzzle out of your head. Important: spend the time needed to do these exercises. I have read or listened to a million (okay, maybe not a million) personal development books. Many have asked me to engage in activities outside the pages of the book. I have done this with only a few. I can tell you based on this nonscientific study that every single time I've been willing to put in the work, I've gotten back the value of my time, plus some. So if you are not in a place to do this pen-to-paper work now, open your calendar and commit to a later time when you can sit down and do the work.

The second common mistake is that people aren't honest about the pieces of their puzzle. When examining both the life we have and the life we want, often it is difficult for us to be truly honest—even with ourselves. Throw in a sprinkling of our fear patterns—fear about speaking up, taking up too much space, failing, asking for what we need—and sheesh, no wonder it is hard. This is the Authenticity Gap in all its glory.

Here's what I'm asking you to do. Make a commitment right now that you will be honest—but not modest—with yourself as you walk through these chapters. Promise me or yourself or the universe/the divine, you will tell it exactly like it actually, factually is. If it makes you feel better, you never ever have to share what you write down with anyone else, and—if it really makes you feel better—you can burn it when you are done (although I bet you're not going to want to do that).

I am going to say it again—I want you to tell it like it actually, *factually* is. That means that you will need to keep a sharp eye out for your stories. What do I mean by *stories*? I mean the things you believe to be true but that can't be supported objectively and factually. As I lawyer, I like to think about stories as things that couldn't be proven in a court of law. When you are wondering if it's a story, ask yourself: *How can I prove it?* If the answer starts with another person's name or the words *I think* or *I feel*, there's a good chance that it's a story. For example, if your reason for putting career first is because your mom put career first, that's probably a story. In addition, if the answer is "It's true because I feel that way," it also may be a story. For example, if you think you need to put family first because you feel like you will be letting your kids down if you don't—that may or may not be a story. Your feelings have a source, but that source can be either fact or fiction. Your feelings can be based on a past experience that is no longer true, or they can truly fit the current facts. You will need to explore which one.

Let me give you an example from my own list of stories. When we first moved into our newly constructed neighborhood, we discovered our street was super social. Families would gather for parties or driveway bonfires. They'd even attend concerts in big groups, and eventually, they vacationed together. When we first arrived on the scene, we were invited to these social gatherings. We attended a few, but we said no to a lot more. We said no because we simply weren't around that much—not because we didn't want to be included. As time went on, the invitations dwindled. Logically, this made sense— who is going to keep inviting someone who never shows up? But the seventh grader in me, whose biggest fear was being left out because she wasn't cool enough, saw things differently. Each Facebook post full of smiling faces was a reminder to that part of me that she didn't fit in, that she wasn't accepted.

But, friends, this wasn't real—this was a story. The fact was, we weren't invited because we didn't show up. And if I'm being really honest, we didn't show up because we were busy with family activities, but also because we weren't making it a priority. The story was that we weren't accepted, the fact was that we were *choosing* not to be. Once I reached this mental turning point, I was able to recognize that some people on our street were friends, with whom a relationship was important to me, and some were just neighbors—really amazing, awesome, wonderful neighbors. And that was fine. It was fine with me and it was fine with them. I reached out to the people whose friendships I valued, and I was honest with them. I explained why we said no to invitations: that it wasn't about them; it was about us. I did this so that their rejection story—if it existed—could have some facts to work with. I also let them know I valued their friendship and that if they were open to it, I wanted to find more time and other ways for us to connect and build our friendship. In this way, I was able to distinguish the stories from the facts. Keep this in the back of your head as you take inventory of your current situation.

ACTION STEP:
TAKE STOCK

Now that we've examined potential bumps in the road, it's time to take stock. It's time to understand all the actual pieces of your current puzzle. Looking at where you are in your current season is vital to knowing what you already have.

I invite you to complete this exercise in whatever way makes sense to you. I am a big fan of Post-it notes because they can be moved around. If, however, you prefer lists or mind maps, or some other format entirely, use what feels best to you. Just use something visible and tangible, please. And hold on to it, you will need the work you do here for later action steps.

Step One: Write down what you are spending your time and energy on (not what you don't but should, or what you really want to be doing) in this season.

You likely have the start to this list from your work defining your season in the last chapter. This list should not be too broad (e.g., marriage), but it also should not be so specific that it's overwhelming (e.g., text with spouse, talk to spouse at noon, watch TV with spouse in the evening). Aim for something in the middle (e.g. daily communication with spouse and time spent with spouse).

Please also note, I said time *and* energy. It's not enough to go through your calendar and make note of what's on your schedule. I also want you to think about the things you spend your emotional energy on. If you are lying awake at night worried about debt, that goes on your list. If you are spending time during lunch thinking about that broken friendship, add it to the list. If you walk around feeling guilty about something, put it on the list. Similarly, if you end each day meditating or journaling about gratitude, add it to the list. Or if you find your mind wandering during your commute, thinking about how much you love your job, put that on the list. The idea is to capture where your energy—physical and emotional—is going right now.

Step Two: Look at the list you've created and ask yourself: What isn't on this list already that I currently spend time or energy on?

Add those things to the list. Keep asking yourself this question until you can't come up with any more answers. Don't skip this step. There is something you missed the first time around. I promise. Give yourself the silence and space needed to discover it.

Step Three: Ask yourself: What's something that I thought about adding to this list but didn't? Or what is something that I know I should add to this list (because it does take my time and energy) but I don't want to?

Add those things. And maybe also underline them. They might be things you want to pay special attention to later because they either need more of your time and energy or they need to be subtracted entirely.

Step Four: Take a look at each item on this list. Ask yourself: How do I know this is true?

Some will be easy. For example, if "Weekly date nights" is on your list and you go on weekly date nights, then it's true. But if that same "Weekly date nights" is just something in your calendar that doesn't actually happen, then take it off the list for now, please. If you are carrying guilt or some other emotional energy around the fact that it doesn't happen, update it to something like "Guilt for missed weekly date nights" or "Frustration about missed weekly date nights."

Extra Credit (because who doesn't love extra credit?): Be grateful.

Before you do anything else, take a few minutes and think about what you are grateful for or proud of from your list. Circle it, underline it, highlight it—just make a note of it. Then say some words of thanks or even reach out to someone else to share your gratitude.

While this step isn't required, I highly encourage it. If your life isn't where you want it to be right now, this exercise may have brought up some uncomfortable emotions. Gratitude is a powerful tool in these moments—it's virtually impossible to be in a state of gratitude and hold on to any negative emotion. Moreover, there is no better platform for change than appreciating where you are today.

In front of you, you now have a physical picture—in black and white, or maybe a pretty color—of how you are spending your time and energy. Looking at that picture might make you feel accomplished or satisfied. It also might make you feel overwhelmed because there is a lot you don't really want there or that you are supposed to be doing but just haven't been able to get to. Whatever you are feeling, it's allowed. And more exciting, we are about to move into a series of chapters full of opportunities for you to think about how you want to change the picture.

Chapter 4

CREATING YOUR MAP—DREAMS

This chapter is for the dreamers. This is where you get to think about what a happier life would look like in this season and possibly the next. Here, we add some new and exciting pieces to your puzzle. But don't worry pragmatists, your chapter is up next. In that chapter, we will also explore the edges of your puzzle—the limits and constraints that actually exist. Since we are going to get there eventually, I hope this means that pragmatists can free themselves up to dream a little first. Dreamers, I'm going to ask you to compromise later.

As a lawyer, professionally trained in risk mitigation and analysis, it's not easy for me to dream. Because limits come so naturally to me, it is sometimes difficult to think without them. In fact, it was the inability to think beyond limits that kept me trapped in a job that was not making me happy for over a year after my bathtub moment. I simply couldn't wrap my head around the possibility of a career that freed me to be more present as a mother but also to continue to do what I wanted to do as a lawyer. Despite what the female partners in my firm's DC office had suggested, litigators didn't go part time in the early 2000s. And I didn't want to start fresh as a different breed of lawyer. I look back at that time now—with the more expansive perspective fifteen years has given me—and I recognize I had so many options. I just couldn't give myself the space to see them all. A big part of my myopia was being afraid to let go of what I thought other people thought I should be doing. If someone had given me permission to engage in a wide-open, no-edges description of the life I wanted to be living right then, I think I could have gotten clearer much faster. It might not have taken a life-threatening pregnancy loss to wake me up to my own happiness.

I use some version of this exercise with almost all my clients. Some clients find it easy to dream—they are natural visionaries. Other clients find it hard to dream beyond the edges of the life they are living. The real magic happens when you truly allow yourself to dream without limits. When you truly allow yourself to name the parts of your dreams that seem a bit out of reach or slightly inconsistent with the life you've lived so far.

Consider Nicole. Nicole was less than a decade into a career in advertising. When we began our work together, her current job wasn't going so great. She was just a year into a shift from account management to the creative side of project management. She still had a lot to learn but wasn't sure she even wanted to learn it. She thought a switch into a slightly different aspect of marketing might be warranted. She wanted coaching help and accountability in figuring out whether this slight adjustment was the right one for her. We started by exploring whether she should consider other areas or careers—she was resolute that marketing and advertising were the only sandboxes she wanted to play in. We spent several sessions building a research, networking, and preliminary job-search plan. As we discussed next steps, Nicole still didn't seem excited or happy. I asked her, "You've made a lot of progress, you've begun making connections in this new field, but you don't seem very excited, am I reading that right?"

She agreed. She was not feeling particularly excited and was discouraged by her own lack of excitement. So I asked her, "What really lights you up? What do you do that you get really excited about?" Her answer: "Vegetarian cooking." She admitted that if she had the freedom to do anything she wanted, she would own a vegetarian restaurant. To be clear, I had also asked her this question at the beginning of our work together, but—in retrospect—her answer had been limited to what she enjoyed in advertising and marketing. She couldn't go beyond the limits of her current reality until she finally realized that was where excitement, happiness, and joy lived. At the end of our short work together, Nicole had not opened a vegetarian restaurant, but her horizons had expanded in a substantial and meaningful way. And that is what this exercise is really about—moving past the limits of your current life to find the places where additional joy lives.

Because I recognize that this type of dreaming doesn't come naturally to everyone, I ask you to consider truly embracing the puzzle analogy with me here. Instead of thinking of your happiness as a problem to be solved, what would happen if you approached it as a puzzle to be assembled? For most of us, that little shift allows us to bring a part of our creative, analytical selves to the party. As you consider how you'd like your current season to look, invite this part of you to the discussion.

For this exercise, have handy the work you did to identify and take stock of your current season, from previous chapters.

ACTION STEP:
REIMAGINE YOUR CURRENT SEASON

In this activity, you will describe the happiest version of your current season. In particular, consider what you would *have* or *be* if you were living a priority-aligned life which allowed you to do less and be more. This is not the time to consider practical constraints, this is the time to dream—to let your heart and your soul ask for their deepest desires. This is hard for some people—so if it feels hard to you that is okay. You can do hard things. Being honest in this exercise is a meaningful step to overcoming any Authenticity Gap that might be getting in the way of your current happiness.

When I use this exercise with clients, sometimes we work through all the areas of their lives using the list below, other times we focus on one or two areas. Because living a happier life includes the whole thing, explore as many categories as you can. Finally, if a category is missing or these categories don't feel right to you, create your own. I'll never know. Potential categories include: career, health, financial, spiritual, family (up, down, and sideways), relationships, friendships, intellectual life, and physical space.

Here again, I invite you to use a format that works for you—list, mind map, picture, something else. It's your call: as long as it's visible, tangible, and you can understand what it means, it's fair game. The instructions for this exercise are short and sweet—but please recognize the exercise itself will take some time, effort, and energy on your part. This exercise is a critical building block for the rest of your work in this book. Hold on to the work you do here so you can review it during future activities.

Step One: For each area of your life, what do you want to have or be in this current season?

Start by reviewing the taking stock exercise you did last chapter. Take what is working and include it here. If some parts aren't exactly how you'd like them, include them with the upgrades you'd like to see. For example, if you are already in a committed relationship but you want to feel even more connected, you might write something like: "Deeper connection in my partnership." Or if you have a job that you like, but want greater opportunity, you might write something like: "Stay in current job but add X, Y, and Z projects or responsibilities."

Next, in this step of the exercise, you have my permission to dream. Be big and be bold. Really take the time to think about what you want. Add to this picture all the pieces of the puzzle you don't yet have, but know you want or need in order to be happier.

This list doesn't need to be exhaustive or highly specific. You can simply write general categories and some supporting concepts. For example, your list might include things like:

Happy marriage—weekly date nights, feeling greater connection, and having fun

Promotion at work—move to VP level, seat at the leadership table, respected expert

Spiritual health—connected with the divine, meditate regularly, regular personal development

THE HAPPINESS RECIPE   43

Remember, this is your list, there are no wrong answers and you can add to it or change it at any time.

Finally, if addressing *all* the areas of your life feels like too much, you can start by focusing on just one or two at a time.

Step Two: What didn't you include in step one because you don't think it's possible?

Remember, no edges here! Even if it seems like a long shot, please include it. You can even blame me for making you do it. It's fine. Dreaming of that promotion, business growth, a new relationship, or an exciting adventure? Write it down.

Step Three: What didn't you include in step one because you are afraid to want it?

I'm betting there is still something you've omitted. Something you are afraid to want. Something you haven't ever said to anyone. Include it—even though it might feel scary. This isn't a contract, it's simply an exploration exercise.

This might be the first place you see your limiting beliefs come up. For example, as I told you, when I finally said out loud that I wanted to be a coach, my limiting beliefs roared in like a freight train. I thought things like: *I am not good enough to coach other people, I've made mistakes as a leader in the past, so who would want to listen to me*, and *I don't look like a coach* (yeah, that's a weird one—but it was there, and I'm all about authentic transparency). You know what? I put "Being an awesome coach with awesome clients" on the list anyway. Because that's what I wanted and what mattered to my happiness. And when I did that, I knew

I would need to confront those beliefs head on to make it happen. If you've got a freight train worth of limiting beliefs coming up here, too, don't worry, you will have the opportunity to bust through them in part II. Just put the thing on your list and make a note of what is making it difficult for you to claim it.

Awesome. I am so excited about the work you've done so far and what's to come for you. This is a good place to stop and really take in the vision you've just outlined. Feel what it would be like to live this way—sooner rather than later. What would work feel like? What would home feel like? What would your relationships feel like? How would you feel about yourself? We are about to dive into practicalities, but, for a moment, really soak in the feel of a happier *right now*. Enjoy it and get excited—because you're about to create it.

Chapter 5

DEFINING YOUR MAP—EDGES

I appreciate you allowing yourself to dream expansively about the happiest version of your current season. I hope you experienced fun and joy as you considered what it would feel like to live a life built that way. By now, you have probably noticed I'm nothing if not practical, and that's what this chapter is all about. It's about finding the edges of your current-season dreams. To be clear, I am going to ask you to edit your vision, *but* not to discard anything that truly matters to you. This is your recipe. Keep anything that fuels a happier *right now*. Our editing will focus on ensuring your dreams are yours—not someone else's; belong in this season—not the next; and are possible—subjectively and contextually.

When I dreamed my current season a couple of months ago, my list included things like:

- Freedom: financial freedom, geographic freedom, and the freedom to control my own time.

- Service: doing work to help others, ability to give freely of both my time and my money.
- Health: be present, gracefully active, and nourishing my body and soul on a daily basis.
- Active social life: find my people, go out more.
- Debt-free: pay off all debt, including my mortgage.

But even my list contained some common traps: pieces in this season's puzzle were really for next season; some pieces represented other people's shoulds rather than my own; and some pieces just weren't possible in this season. In other words, I had a pile of puzzle pieces with no edges. Before taking action, I needed to eliminate pieces that fell outside the edges of this season's puzzle.

To resolve this dilemma, I first identified what I felt I *should* have but didn't really want. Don't get it twisted, it's not always easy to see—but once you see it, it's a game changer. For me, the biggest piece in this category was "active social life" and everything that went with it. When I made this list, I was staring down the barrel of a spring and summer of being on the road almost every weekend for kids travel basketball and being apart from my husband almost all of those weekends. I don't say that to complain, but to set the stage. I realized that even if I wanted to go to every concert, happy hour, or neighborhood gathering, I simply couldn't. Rather than being disappointed, I was relieved. Though I put it on my dream list, it wasn't what I really wanted—it was what I thought I was supposed to want. It's what social media and my community told me I needed to be accepted, loved, and part of a group. My solution was to recognize that what I wanted was to pour more energy into the authentic friendships I had and ensure I devoted time to enjoying them when I could. As a result, my puzzle piece was transformed from "active social life" into "cultivate authentic friendships."

Next, I identified what didn't belong to this season, but rather to the next season (or maybe beyond). The one that jumped out right away was "geographic freedom." I have a real and valid dream of equally dividing my year into time at the beach, at home, and in the mountains somewhere. I'm not relieved I can't actualize this in my current season. I am committed to achieving it someday. But my current season is defined by business building and parenting high schoolers. Even if my job allowed me to work from the beach whenever I wanted (which it basically does), I wouldn't want to leave my teenagers for months at a time (and they have no interest in living a nomadic lifestyle). So this dream is on hold until next season. I've already started and will continue to build the foundation. Knowing I want this is relevant to the choices I make now, but it's not more important than those things that will directly impact this season's happiness.

Finally, I identified the pieces of my dream puzzle that simply aren't possible. For me, that is to pay off all debt including my mortgage. A note: possibility in this exercise is entirely subjective and contextual. Anything is possible. I could focus all my energy on earning sufficient money to pay off my mortgage, whatever it takes. In that sense, this dream is possible. But given what else I want right now—including the freedom to build the business of my dreams—I recognize it's acceptable to carry some smart debt (for me smart debt is debt with an interest rate lower than the return I can get in the market). Rather than seek to be debt-free by the end of this business-building season, I edited this element to "be financially secure"—to be able to service the smart debt I had, pay down some less-smart debt, and live a comfortable lifestyle.

All these little tweaks to my list were important in defining the perimeter of this season's happiness puzzle. The changes I made put me one step closer to translating what I wanted into actionable lifestyle changes. Below is an exercise to help you do the same.

ACTION STEP:
FIND THE EDGES

I invite you to revisit what you created last chapter in the "Reimagine Your Current Season" activity and make some edits—removing or revising your puzzle pieces as appropriate. After you complete this activity you should have a concise list of what you want in your current season—the ingredients for this season's happiness recipe.

Step One: Letting go of other people's shoulds.

Let's tackle the hardest one first. I am betting you have pieces in your puzzle you don't really want there, but you think you should have because someone else has told you that's how it's done. It's time to get honest about those pieces and take them out. This is an opportunity to head the Authenticity Gap off at the pass. You shouldn't spend any more time or energy working to achieve things you don't even want, right?

Take a look at your list. For each thing on your list ask yourself the following questions:

What about this thing is important to me?

Who else in my life thinks this is important?

Do I think it is important?

How disappointed would I be if I couldn't have this?

If I don't want exactly this, is there an edited or related version of this that I do want?

Walk through these questions for things you already have and things you want. You might discover that some things you have—and thought you wanted to carry forward— are other people's shoulds. And that you want to release them.

Based on your answers to these questions, remove the item or edit it as appropriate.

Step Two: Move it to next season.

Next, consider what pieces in your dream puzzle aren't part of this season. It is easy to get ahead of yourself. We are trained to think about happiness as a future state— some distant horizon where we'll finally have everything we want and the freedom to enjoy it. Therefore, it's not surprising that when you take time to envision what you'd like to achieve, you add things that belong in the more distant future. This is an opportunity to move them off the list for now. You aren't abandoning them—they can stay on your dream list and be part of your long-term vision. You are simply recognizing they aren't going to be achieved now, so you aren't going to invest a bunch of energy trying to make them happen in this season. Instead, you'll focus on what you can do to make this season happier.

Review your list and ask:

When do I want this?

If your answer is anything other than "right now" (in this season), move this to a future-season list. Remember, relocating that dream doesn't mean you're abandoning it. Rather, you are acknowledging that this isn't something you want and need in this season, but something you'd like to build toward and achieve in a future season.

Step Three: Remove the impossible.

Keep in mind, *possible* is subjective and contextual. Something (or maybe more than one thing) in your pile of pieces isn't possible—defined subjectively and contextually. You can let it go. You might be letting it go forever or simply for now. Either way, release it. If you continue to put energy toward it, you will only further exacerbate your Authenticity Gap and your Physical Energy Gap and any related unhappiness. If you truly want it but the *fear* of impossibility is what you're really feeling, don't let go of this piece just yet. Leave it on the list and make a note. You can engage with that fear in part II to discover what it is telling you. If you find it's simply a fear of growing or of success—you may find a way to keep that piece in your puzzle.

When tackling this step, don't let your fearful self lead with its "I just can't do it"—instead, invite your practical self to say, "This is not really possible (in this season or ever) and I accept that." Review your list and ask:

Is this possible in this season?

If the answer is no, consider removing it from your list. Before you make a final decision, ask yourself: *Am I taking this off because I don't need it/it's not possible or because*

I'm scared that I can't do it? If it's the latter, leave it on the list.

I hope you are walking out of this chapter with a clear—or at least clearer—picture of what you want in your current season. It's taken honesty and effort to get here. Take a minute and see if you can get excited about where you are headed. Feel what it would be like if this picture were really your life. Next, we'll connect these pieces of your puzzle to the actions you need to achieve them, with a pit stop at feelings and beliefs.

PART II

THE EMOTIONAL ENERGY GAP

I want to tell you the story of two women who are both highly capable and intelligent and have achieved great things. They are both pretty clear on what they want and need to be happy and have taken serious steps to close their Authenticity Gap. In short, they both want more than what they have today. The first woman, believing that to have more you need to do more, just keeps adding to her list. Soon, her days are full to the point of overwhelm. She wakes up each day worried over what she must do and fitfully falls asleep, guilt ridden over what she didn't do that she should have. Because she wants more, she says yes to every opportunity—*no* just isn't in her vocabulary. Because she knows she's capable, she rarely asks for help. Her friends describe her as a superhero—they can't believe how much she can do and often wonder how she does it.

When things go right, she worries about what could go wrong—and when things are really good, she finds herself waiting for the other shoe to drop. She's heard that feeling good leads to good things happening, so she avoids negative feelings any time she can—she thinks she's being optimistic and joyful. She accomplishes by sheer force. She sets goals and achieves them *except* when things don't work perfectly. When things don't work and she stumbles, she's quick to set down the goal and move on to something else. She has a lot of what she wants but much of what she has drains her energy, resources, and time. She's tired, overwhelmed, and out of control—despite all her efforts to control the outcomes. And she's over it.

Now meet the second woman. Like the first, she is clear on what she wants. But unlike the first, she knows she doesn't need to do more to be more. She recognizes she must do *more* of what matters and *less* of the rest. She says no. A lot. It's hard sometimes, but she still does it. She gets a lot done and works hard but doesn't often struggle because she is working on things that matter to her. She knows she wants to feel good; so instead of worrying about what might go wrong, she spends time thinking about how it will feel if it goes right. She asks for help—often and from a diverse supporting cast—because she knows that humans need other humans to be happy. She knows she's not meant to carry her life alone. She sees all feelings as necessary, so she's no longer afraid of the difficult ones. She knows they will come and how to honor them when they do. She's in control of her life and her choices. She knows where she can exert control and where to surrender. She is not perfect at any of this, but she is pretty good. And pretty good—not perfect—makes for a mostly guilt-free, mostly happy, and mostly satisfied life.

What if I told you the only core difference between these two women is their feelings and beliefs? Yes, their actions are different, their days look and feel very different. But guess what's driving that difference? Their emotional energy. How do I know? Because both of these women are me. That first woman, she's where I started. And she's where I stayed for a *long time.* I was clear on what I wanted. And I took that clarity right into *making it happen.* I didn't stop to really assess whether brute force was actually my only option. That second woman arrived on scene after a lot of personal growth and reflection. Most importantly, she arrived when I realized that change requires more than clarity, desire, and action—change requires understanding your beliefs, feelings, and the role your nervous system plays in supporting or halting your progress.

This is where we will start in part II—with your nervous system. I want you to understand that your nervous system plays a significant role in creating your Emotional Energy Gap. And I want you to see that you can't set yourself up for success when your beliefs and feelings don't match the action and outcomes you want. Once you have a basic understanding of your nervous system and how to use it, you'll look at what beliefs and feelings you might need to shift to make lasting change. From there, you'll learn myriad ways to shift these beliefs and feelings. We will go through the most common barrier beliefs I have encountered in my life and work, and I will offer you a breakthrough behavior for each. If you are an action taker, you may be feeling pretty antsy. After all, you have in front of you this vision of a better right now, and you want to make it happen! I get it. I really do. But I promise, building a solid bridge between desire and action with supportive feelings and beliefs will help you jump into part III and make it happen for good in a way you'll actually enjoy this time.

Chapter 6

YOUR INDICATOR LIGHT

As I've mentioned, the Emotional Energy Gap often gets missed. You've missed it if you've ever jumped straight from desire to action. This gap is the biggest culprit of failed attempts, repeated start-and-stop loops, and procrastination. That's because this gap has an extraordinarily effective partner in crime: your nervous system.

I am not going to teach you the intricacies of nervous system science. Many wonderful authors have done so in other books. I simply want to give you a foundational understanding of the role that your nervous system can play in keeping you stuck and how you can use it to support your growth. If you find this stuff interesting or want to know more, I've included a few resources at the end of this book to support your continued learning. The nervous system is complex, but the description below is deliberately simple.

I am giving you this high-level nervous system overview because I think it will help you understand two important

things. First, you'll realize that your nervous system sometimes operates on outdated rules in an effort to keep you safe.
The problem: it often keeps you safe from things that don't
actually pose a danger to you—like growth and change. Over
the course of your life, and especially in childhood, your nervous system has learned how to keep you safe. These learnings
become rules (or patterns) of nervous system response that
stay with you and influence your behavior even when circumstances have changed. These patterns play a significant role in
your Emotional Energy Gap.

Second, you'll learn how to get your nervous system to
become both your early-warning system and your ally as you
begin living a more priority-aligned life. Nervous system messages from your body to your brain far outnumber those that
go from your brain to your body. This means that you can use
the nervous system messages from your body as an early indicator that your nervous system thinks you are headed into
dangerous territory. In effect, you have an indicator light that
lets you know when you are about to confront the Emotional
Energy Gap. You just need to know how to interpret it.

Like me, you probably learned the basics of your nervous
system in high school or college biology courses. Let's refamil-
iarize you here. You have a nervous system and one of its primary jobs is to keep you safe. Loosely defined, in this context,
safety means your ability to have your most basic needs met
(like food, shelter, and physical safety) and to feel connected
to others. From your nervous system's perspective, an unsafe
situation is where you risk losing something you need to sur-
vive or not being connected to people who matter to you—in
childhood this is likely your parents.

You probably know that when your nervous system perceives a threat, it gets triggered and moves you into fight-or-
flight response. In our lives, things happen to us, with us, or
around us that our nervous system perceives as unsafe. In

other words, when your nervous system senses a threat to your safety (real or simply perceived) it compels you to do what it thinks will keep you safe. Considering this, it's not surprising, then, that your nervous system can be triggered by trauma (where you are actually terribly unsafe). In the context of trauma, it explains why people are triggered into fight, flight, or freeze when something occurs that looks, sounds, or feels similar to their traumatic event. My focus here is not trauma. My focus is on more everyday experiences. This same nervous system response can also be triggered by experiences more subtle than trauma. When this happens, and it is significant or continuous, your nervous system spots a pattern. And in response to this pattern, your nervous system develops a rule. It concludes, *I don't want to do X, because X means I am unsafe—I will not get my needs met. So when I am asked to do X—or something that looks like we are headed toward X—I'm going to sound the alarm and, if necessary, trigger fight, flight, or freeze so that you don't do X.* Similarly, your nervous system also observes positive connections and may feel unsafe when it perceives there is a risk of losing that positive connection. For example, it may conclude, *When I do Y, I receive love. I want to keep doing Y, and I won't permit the opposite of Y, because I risk losing connection if I do.*

This matters because when your nervous system is triggered into fight, flight, or freeze response, your brain's functioning is not optimal for decision-making. Often in these triggered states, you make decisions you later regret, say things you don't mean, procrastinate, withdraw, get angry, or maybe you quit. In essence, when your nervous system learns that a certain behavior or situation results in a lack of safety—pain, neglect, or even disconnection—it creates a rule that reads something like: *Don't do X, it's not safe.* And then it does everything it can to convince your brain not to do X.

Let's look at a couple of examples. Imagine a young boy. He has all his physical needs (food, shelter, etc.) met, and he generally feels connected to and loved by his parents. However, whenever he throws a tantrum—getting forceful, loud, and angry—his parents reprimand him. This kind of over-the-top display of emotion is not acceptable behavior in their house. This response can easily get categorized in the child's nervous system as something like *Anger is bad* or even *My anger is bad*. It gets categorized this way, even in an immature nervous system, because one of our most basic needs, especially as a child, is connection or love. When his parents punish this behavior, his nervous system gets a message like: *If you behave that way, you will not be connected or loved.*

Now consider a young girl. She also has all her physical needs met. Her parents want to give her wings, so they repeatedly reward her for her independence. When she solves a problem on her own, they heap on the praise. When she does her homework without help, they are thrilled. When she does ask for help, there's no corresponding negative reaction—though they sometimes ask her to figure it out on her own first. And when she does, it's a party. So her nervous system learns, *When I do things for myself, I am connected and loved.* And it learns: *I don't want to ask for help, because then I have less connection and love.*

The parents in both examples have done nothing wrong. Most loving parents don't intend to send these absolute messages when addressing behavior, but they are sending a message to an unsophisticated audience—a child—who isn't yet capable of subtleties in categorization and who is largely reliant on them to get their needs met.

This energetic artifact then lives in this child's nervous system and becomes the basis for their attachment patterns (or coping mechanisms). These patterns aren't good or bad, they just are—and they are unique to your experiences in childhood and beyond. Translating that into simple English—your nervous system may have learned: *My anger is bad and to receive love* (which is all any of us really want, especially as children), *I need to avoid showing my anger,* or maybe even *I need to avoid asking for what I need.* Or it may have learned, *I get the most connection when I am independent, so I will try to do it all on my own. It is bad to ask for help because I will risk disconnection. And being disconnected is unsafe.* These are just a few, perhaps oversimplified, examples. If you want to dig deeper into your attachment pattern work, I highly recommend finding a trauma-informed practitioner to work with. It is my hope, however, that you understand the basic premise: your nervous system learns to anticipate unsafe situations based on its past experiences.

Unlike your cellphone operating system, your nervous system doesn't get regular, automatic updates while you sleep. Instead, these old rules persist and your nervous system continues to apply them in an effort to keep you safe. This response has served a purpose in the past—it has kept you safe. Many nervous system responses are totally necessary and shouldn't be changed—like *Don't touch the hot stove* or *Don't play in traffic.* But if you want to change and grow, you will need to consider the role nervous system programming plays in your behavior and whether the rules you carry are still serving you.

For example, if you learned as a child that *anger is bad* and *to receive love you need to avoid showing your anger,* as an adult you might find yourself struggling to express yourself in difficult or tense situations. You probably don't still need a nervous system rule that says *anger is always bad,* but you may need some boundaries around anger or an updated rule that allows you to express it in a constructive way. Similarly, if you grew up believing that independence was king, it might feel scary and uncomfortable to ask for support. If you identify with this, you may want to explore asking for help more often, but you won't want to abandon your independence entirely. In addition, as you approach each situation in which your nervous system sees a threat to your safety, you likely will feel some physical sensations.

Good news: you have an early-warning system that indicates when one of your nervous system's rules is triggered, providing real-time data to your nervous system about whether the perceived threat is an actual threat. I call this your Indicator Light. Much like the Check Engine light on a car, it's a sign your brain will soon function at less-than-optimal levels. Knowing this allows you to reset or remove and reboot. You can provide additional data to help regulate your nervous system's response *or* you can remove yourself and revisit the situation after you've calmed down.

How can you find this magical Indicator Light? That requires a little bit of work. Here's how it goes. This light lives in your body. Yes, in your body. That's because, you may recall, the nervous system pathways from body to brain far outweigh those from brain to body. Said another way, your body is sensing a threat and communicating that to your brain—not the other way around. Thus, physical symptoms can be nervous system indicator lights that you're entering "unsafe" territory. Often, you'll experience physical symptoms before you are even aware of being in a triggered state—before your brain has a chance to understand what is going on. For example, you might feel a lump in your throat, or you might feel sick to your stomach. You might get sweaty palms or have twitchy legs. This is good news. If you can deepen the brain-to-body connection and begin to notice when physical symptoms consistent with a triggered nervous system arise, you'll recognize when your brain is about to be functioning at less-than-optimal levels. You can get curious about what is going on and feed the nervous system additional context and information to indicate that you are actually safe—despite your nervous system's past experiences. Now let's dive into finding *your* Indicator Light.

ACTION STEP:
FIND YOUR LIGHT

It's time to familiarize yourself with your Indicator Light so you can spot moments when your nervous system is triggering a flight, fight, or freeze state and take steps to restore a calmer, more effective brain state. A quick note about these various states—I've discussed them a little and you probably have some ideas about what they look like, but I want to expand your view a little bit. A fight state can look like anxiety, rude or sarcastic responses, or straight-up fighting. A flight state can look like leaving a situation, ignoring a problem, or refusing to engage. A freeze state can look like inaction, procrastination, disconnection, or even dissociation.

HISTORICAL FOUNDATION

Think of a time in recent memory where you were in fight, flight, or freeze response.

No need to revisit the biggest trauma in your life or an unhappy moment from your childhood. Instead, consider a time in recent memory when your brain wasn't functioning optimally. It could be a fight with your partner, a contentious conversation with a family member or coworker, or even a run-in with a terrible driver.

When that happened, what were you feeling physically?

You might be able to answer this question right away, or you might find this question a bit unusual. But do me a favor and give it a try—think about any physical symptoms you had. Maybe your heart was racing, your legs were bouncing, or you felt a lump in your throat. Maybe you were fighting back tears, clenching your fists, or feeling something in the pit of your stomach. There is no wrong or right answer. Your Indicator Light is uniquely your own.

It may be helpful to answer the questions above about a couple of different situations so that you can get a good understanding of your Indicator Light.

ONGOING OBSERVATION

Because most of us don't listen to our bodies regularly, we benefit from practicing this new skill. To deepen your understanding of your Indicator Light, observe how your nervous system reacts over the next ten to fourteen days. Now that you've identified some of your physical symptoms, keep an eye out for times these symptoms come up. You can track these however it makes sense to you. I recommend taking time at least once a day to jot down these moments. Note what was happening, how you were feeling, and where you were feeling it. If you do this exercise over a period of time, you will uncover some patterns. What I've discovered: I get forehead tension when a situation is escalating into conflict and I am not ready to be confrontational, my upper gut tightens when I'm about to get vulnerable or ask for help, and my heart pounds when I'm afraid of letting someone else down.

As we move forward, I will point out times where I've seen people's Indicator Light turn on and show you how to work through the resistance that may ensue. If you find your nervous system is frequently triggered or is creating a barrier to your progress, I strongly encourage you to dig deeper and enlist support.

In sum, I hope our nervous system exploration has helped you become more aware that your nervous system was programmed at a young age under different circumstances than you face today. Furthermore, this programming likely contributes to your Emotional Energy Gap and has stopped you from making desired changes in the past. Being aware of this programming can allow you to make lasting change. With Indicator Light awareness, you can now spot moments in your life—particularly as you walk this path of change—when your nervous system perceives a safety threat. Identifying the physical symptoms of a triggered nervous system warns you that, soon, your brain will not be capable of making the best decisions. If you can notice these Indicator Light signals in your body, you can provide additional information to confirm or refute the perception of a threat. Ultimately, you are able to employ your nervous system as an ally in your growth rather than a barrier that keeps you stuck. Keep an eye on your Indicator Light as you take a closer look at your feelings and beliefs in the next chapter.

Chapter 7

BRIDGE FROM IDEAS TO ACTION—PUTTING THE PIECES TOGETHER

Get excited because it's about to get good. In this chapter, we will explore how to move from idea to action—using the bridge of beliefs and feelings. Here, you will start to close your Emotional Energy Gap. Here, you will begin to assemble your puzzle. Here, you will start to see the images that represent your happiness and ease begin to take shape. Here, you are going to reverse engineer your happiness by considering what you need to believe and feel to have what you want in this season of your life. I can unequivocally assure you that some of these beliefs and feelings will be new. If you already believed them and felt them, you wouldn't be here. Because they are new, they might be uncomfortable. Remember, discomfort means you are moving and growing. Moreover, in the ensuing chapters, we'll work with the most common barrier beliefs and the breakthrough behaviors you can use to overcome them.

Usually, when considering what we want to achieve or have, we jump to what we need to *do* to get it. We go from desire straight to action, without considering whether we have the necessary infrastructure of beliefs and feelings to support our success. Now is the time to evaluate your foundational infrastructure. This will help you identify where you might need further growth to support your action. Instead of *doing*, in the traditional sense, you might need to work on shifting a *feeling* or *belief*. We'll explore what to do if you encounter a roadblock in future chapters—for now, let's start building a bridge that will connect what you want with what you need to do.

Addressing your Emotional Energy Gap in this way is critically important to your ultimate success. There is a reason you don't already have what you want—perhaps you don't have the beliefs or feelings needed to support the action required. That is what happened to James. James recently started a new client-facing job after moving through several similar positions at different companies over a few-year span. James wanted to make a good impression on his new internal and external clients. Though he was working hard and considered himself a capable writer, James began receiving feedback that his written communications didn't instill confidence in his client base.

In our first coaching session, he wanted to focus on his written communication style to address this feedback. As James and I talked, it became clear that he didn't have confidence in himself. It was no wonder, then, that he wasn't communicating confidently with others. On one hand, James felt he was capable and skilled. He had objective evidence that supported this feeling. I asked James to describe what he wanted his clients to believe about him. He wanted them to view him as an industry expert who knew the current trends and how to apply them to their specific situations. Sounds reasonable, right? Then I asked

James if he believed those things about himself. After a long pause, James told me he thought he did but wasn't always sure. He described how a handful of previous job experiences had undermined his confidence.

Now James knew what we needed to work on together. Before working on his writing style, he needed to work on his confidence. As James built his self-confidence, that strong, assured voice came through in his writing without any additional effort on his part. Moreover, his confident attitude spread into other areas of his professional and personal life. Had he only focused on changing his writing style, he would have missed the opportunity to remove a big barrier to his future success.

Because many high-potential high achievers are often action driven or solutions oriented, they frequently jump right in to fix a problem. As I told you, for a long time that is how I behaved. It's a great approach if you are sure you've identified what needs fixing. If, like James, you've relied on other people to tell you what needs fixing without any self-reflection, you could miss unlocking a completely unanticipated category or level of future success. Taking time to consider if your feelings and beliefs align with your goals is worth its weight in gold. Below is a process to explore this so you can close your Emotional Energy Gap.

If you did a complete map of your desired current season last chapter, continue to work with the whole list. While it may take a bit more time, this full picture will help you do the prioritization work in the coming chapters. If, on the other hand, you want to focus on only one or two areas, that is your prerogative—just work with what you have.

ACTION STEP:
BUILD YOUR BRIDGE

Here again, the directions are simple, but the work isn't necessarily easy. It's just three steps, but it's deep work. You must discover what you'd feel and believe if you had what you wanted in your current season. Inevitably, some of these feelings and beliefs are going to be new and different. You may feel uncomfortable or notice your Indicator Light turn on. If that happens, it's normal. In fact, it's a great opportunity to befriend your nervous system and remind it—out loud—that you are safe and simply exploring another way of doing things. I usually say something like: "Thank you. I recognize you are trying to keep me safe and you've kept me safe with this strategy in the past. But I'm grown up now, I've got this and I'm going to do this. You are welcome to come along for the ride, but you are not allowed to drive!"

Similarly, it's not uncommon for big emotions to come up—I've experienced this personally and with my clients. It can be super vulnerable to claim the amazing and awesome things you want to feel and the empowering beliefs you need to have, because you're not used to it. Remind yourself that you are allowed to have big feelings. If your feelings get in the way of doing this exercise fully, hop over to chapter 11 for some tools to work with your feelings and then come back here. Finally, remember this is an exploration not a contract. You are not bound by what you write here, unless you want to be.

Step One: Ask yourself: How would I feel if I had what I said I want in my current season?

Really envision what it would feel like to be happy in your current season. For example, last time I did this exercise, I envisioned that if I were "gracefully active," I would feel motivated, strong, comfortable in my own skin. Similarly, a client wanting to gain a seat at the leadership table described feelings of confidence, being heard, and being seen. As you reflect on what you've said you want in your current season, you may have unexpected feelings come up. That is okay. This is an opportunity to check once more that you have captured what you actually want—what actually matters to you—not what you think you should want.

Step Two: Ask yourself: What do I need to believe about myself to have what I want in my current season?

It can be hard and scary to explore the beliefs we need to have to change our feelings and behavior. But it's crucial to closing our Emotional Energy Gap. Sticking with my desire to be "gracefully active," I identified that I would need to believe that I could find an exercise routine I enjoyed, I could follow through on my commitment to move, and I am allowed to take time for myself to make this happen. I suspect you can see what these beliefs stirred up—issues of self-esteem, self-control, and time and energy management. Similarly, my client who wanted to take her career to the next level needed to believe that she was capable, her voice was worth hearing, and, fundamentally, she was good enough. Big stuff.

Sometimes the beliefs you identify will already feel comfortable and true—that's awesome. These feelings and beliefs don't have to be major changes (or changes at all) to go on this list, they just have to support what you are trying to achieve.

Step Three: Identify areas of resistance.

Sometimes you'll write down a belief and immediately think, *Oh, I can't or don't feel that way* or *I'll never believe that.* Circle, underline, or highlight those—the ones that will be hard to feel or believe. Those feelings and barrier beliefs need your attention if you want to take the action required to make you happy in this life season.

It's where the work is needed most, and where you are most likely to see your nervous system's Indicator Light switch on.

In the chapters that follow, I will offer you some action steps for dealing with these specific feelings and barrier beliefs that may have come up for you.

Last time I did this exercise, I was about to launch my coaching business. I was on the brink of telling everyone I knew, whose opinions I cared about, that I was no longer pursuing a traditional big-organization career path. I also planned to go a step further and tell them I could help them figure out how to live happy and successful lives. As I looked at what I needed to feel and believe to do this, one thing jumped off the page, grabbed my heart, and put it firmly in my throat. To take this leap, I needed to believe I was more than good enough to serve as a guide and coach to other people. This was big for me.

Had you asked me three years ago whether, as a general proposition, I thought I was good enough, I would have shared all the ways I rocked. I promise, professional ego has never been a big issue for me. But when it came to holding myself out as an expert, a real tender spot reared its head. It surprised me. It was new and different. I also knew if I wanted to be as happy and successful as I desired, I would need to deal with this gap. Identifying and working with this gap was critical to my current success and happiness (more about that later). Had I launched my business without examining my feelings and beliefs, I might have experienced some degree of happiness, but I would have had this lingering feeling of not being good enough tugging on my nervous system, asking me to play smaller and stay closer to my comfort zone. If I had not confronted this feeling, I wouldn't have written this book—that would have been too big, too bold, and too visible for the part of me that still believed I might not be quite good enough.

Now you have a picture of what you need to believe and feel to have more happiness in your current season. I hope you are feeling a little bit of excitement, a dash of fear, and enough energy to keep you going. You should have a sense of where you might encounter resistance as you step into a more priority-aligned life. You may have identified beliefs and feelings you need to adjust or evolve. Don't let this intimidate you. In the next several chapters, you'll practice the breakthrough behaviors that can shift the feelings and barrier beliefs to support your ultimate happiness. This is an exciting opportunity to be the author of your life. Remember: this is your path; you don't have to do anything more than you want to. But also remember that discomfort and a little fear are signs you are moving and growing.

Chapter 8

BREAKTHROUGH BEHAVIOR #1 BORROWING JOY

I'm going to say it straight—life doesn't need to feel so difficult. The first common barrier belief I want to address is that joy requires suffering. It arises when we believe that life simply can't be this good, that we haven't earned this happiness, or that the other shoe must be about to drop.

Despite what you might think, you don't need to buy joy with suffering. This concept isn't revolutionary—although sometimes when I'm working with clients, and even myself, it can feel that way. Sometimes this barrier belief pops up when it starts to get really good (or, if you are like me, only moderately good). You find yourself waiting for the other shoe to drop, and it inevitably does. Have you ever found yourself in a happy place—things were going well, you had more money, more happiness, or more love than you thought you could (maybe than you thought you deserved)—and then *boom*, something suddenly shifted you into struggle mode? Maybe you had a petty (or not so petty) fight with your significant other. Or maybe you spent that extra money frivolously and found your bank account right back where it started.

Gay Hendricks describes this phenomenon as the "Upper Limit Problem" in his book *The Big Leap*. He posits that we all have an internal regulator switch, and when we get too happy or successful, it gets flipped and we limit ourselves. This is a nervous system trigger, but it's different from those we normally think about. This switch gets flipped when things are going too well. In effect, this trigger occurs when we are afraid (consciously or subconsciously) not of failure, but of success.

This is a symptom of your Emotional Energy Gap—it is your old feelings, beliefs, and patterns popping up. It might sound like: "You don't deserve to be happy" or "It's too good, something bad must be about to happen." Sometimes, however subconsciously, you may find yourself looking for trouble or conflict just because you believe it's inevitable. This is real. But these limits on happiness are learned and can be unlearned. You must be open to shifting your perspective.

I know it sounds weird to say that our nervous system wants to keep us safe from being too happy. But really, it's more like our nervous system wants to keep us safe from the unknown. It would prefer us to keep sailing familiar waters— even if those waters are choppy. Our nervous system lights up when it notices we're going outside our comfort zone, which it perceives as discomfort. This explains why, when things are going well in one area of your life, they might suddenly fall apart in another. Why, for example, when you lose the first ten pounds, you ditch the diet and start eating sugar at every meal again. Why, when you have a great day at work, you come home and get in a fight with your kids or your partner. This is why, when you haven't been living a happy, joy-filled life, it feels weird and potentially uncomfortable when you do. And your nervous system may try to drag or nudge you back into your comfort zone of struggle and hard work.

I still fall victim to this phenomenon sometimes. In fact, recently, I was having an awesome day. It was Saturday after a super productive week. After tie-dyeing and a lovely walk with my daughter that morning, I parked myself on the porch with a book. The sun was shining, the humidity was low, and a gentle breeze blew just enough to keep me cool, but not enough to ruffle the pages of my beach read. I sat, book open in lap, taking in my neighborhood and letting my mind wander. Then I had two thoughts in quick succession. I thought, *I'm happy. In this moment, I couldn't be happier.* This was followed almost immediately by *I can't be* that *happy. I've still got this book to finish. And, oh yeah, that school change for my daughter is looming. And what about that argument I had yesterday.* In less time than a breath, I'd managed to arrest my happiness by being afraid that the other shoe would drop *and* by identifying all the potential shoes. The good news: I've been working on my upper limit problem. I spotted it right away. And in spotting it, I was able to stop it and turn it around, using the technique I describe below.

This technique has been built on decades of experience. I've been a lifelong worrier. I don't usually describe it that way—I usually say I'm a planner. But really, I'm a professional what-if-er. If there were an award or degree, I'd have it. When I was younger, I dealt with anticipated discomfort by evaluating all the worst-case scenarios and figuring out if and how I could manage them. Sometimes I'd become absorbed in the worst-case scenarios to the point of upset. My what-if-ing ranged from the mundane (the play audition that was going to result in total embarrassment, the test I was going to fail, the first date that was going to be terrible, the speech I was going to flop) to the life changing (the college I wasn't getting into, the roommate who I would end up hating, or the job interview that was going to be a total disaster). My relatively levelheaded mother would routinely cut me off during my spinout by saying, "Becky, stop borrowing trouble." What she meant was, stop spending emotional energy on a negative outcome that you aren't even sure is going to happen. My teenage self didn't always appreciate this response. My adult self, on the other hand, not only appreciates this response but says it to her children on the regular. (We really do turn into our parents.)

"Stop borrowing trouble" makes so much sense to me now. As I consider that living a priority-aligned life is essentially about matching your energy to what matters most to you, it's only logical that you shouldn't spend energy on an outcome you don't want. What a waste. Our energy is precious. Not only does my adult self appreciate this reset, I've taken it one step further.

Now I try to avoid borrowing trouble, *and* I find ways to borrow joy instead. Rather than just refraining from spending energy on a not-yet-arrived negative outcome, I recognize that if I'm going to play the what-if game—which seems unavoidable for me—I would rather spend my mental and emotional energy thinking, *What if it all turns out great?* and more importantly, *How will it feel when it does?* As with all shifts in behavior and mindset, it's about progress not perfection. Sometimes I still find myself going down the rabbit hole asking: *What if I fail miserably?* The good news is that now I more easily catch myself and add *What if I succeed?* to the mental conversation.

ACTION STEP:
BORROW JOY

Deploy this practice any time your mind hops on the what-if train. Give it a whirl now, paying particular attention to the thoughts that come up as you consider the shift to a more priority-aligned life.

Ask: As you think about the growth and change you anticipate needing in your life, what are your what-ifs?

This list can be short or long. If making the list seems likely to spin you into a negative what-if spiral, consider a numerical limitation. Only allow yourself three, five, or ten at a time. This works best if you write your answers down. Leave a little space between items or next to your list (I like to use two columns for this activity).

Review: Identify any what-ifs that constitute borrowing trouble.

If it isn't certain (or quickly made certain) and it's negative, it's borrowing trouble. When I do this exercise, pretty much all my what-ifs fit this category. Every so often, however, I come up with a what-if that I can quickly address (e.g., what if the facility is not available when I need it?). This what-if is easily removable—I can take care of answering it with a quick email or phone call—so I ignore it for this next step.

Reframe: Take the first "borrowing trouble" what-if on your list and borrow joy instead.

Rewrite that what-if from one of concern, fear, guilt, or anxiety to one that is positive. Really sit with that positive what-if. Breathe it in. Consider what it will feel like if the positive what-if actually happens. Think about it so much you start to actually feel it. Allow it to become as much a part of you as the original negative what-if.

If it's hard to think about what success might feel like in this particular context, you can always go back to another time when you enjoyed the outcome. Think about those positive feelings. Remember what it felt like when things were good and when you were proud, satisfied, or happy. Really lean into those feelings and then imagine feeling those things in this circumstance. Allow yourself some positive daydreams. You will know you've succeeded when you start to smile at your own thoughts.

The more you practice this exercise, the more easily you can catch yourself starting down the what-if spiral. Next time you start to think, *What if I fail?* make sure you remember to also ask yourself, *What if I succeed?* Give *at least* equal airtime—energetically, conversationally, mentally—to both. In a perfect world, you will turn your full focus to thinking about what happens when it all works out just the way it was meant to.

I want to add a note about the difference between anticipating and preparing for risk and what-if-ing. Remember, I'm a lawyer—I'm trained to identify and mitigate risk. There is a place and time for that, but it is not all the time. As you begin to borrow more joy, the difference between risk mitigation and what-if will become clearer. You'll recognize when you are legitimately protecting yourself against a downside risk versus completely spinning your wheels or spiraling into a zone of bad-outcome energy expenditure.

Leaning into the feeling that everything will turn out perfectly prepares you to live a more priority-aligned life. Like before, moving in this direction can be uncomfortable, and your nervous system might try to guide you back to the way it's always been. Recognize that this is your nervous system mistaking growth for a lack of safety. And ask your nervous system, for now, just to keep an open mind, to allow that there might be a different way of doing things that, while uncomfortable at first, could actually be better. And then embrace what it will feel like when it all turns out just as it should.

Chapter 9

BREAKTHROUGH BEHAVIOR #2 SOURCE JOY

Our next barrier belief is the idea that you need to do more to have more—that happiness only comes from hustle. If you are anything like me, you grew up thinking you need to do more to be more. Work harder and you'd get better grades. Get better grades and you'd get a better job. Work harder in that job, and you'd make more money. And it's not just me who thinks this, consider the traditional employment model—work hard and do what you need to do to make as much money as possible, then retire and enjoy the fruits of your labor. I saw this model firsthand in law firms—hard charge through the associate years for the payoff of partnership. Happiness was important only as an end achievement—partnership or retirement—and wasn't seen or treated as critical during your career.

Here's the thing, hard work might produce some results, but it might not make you happy. I'm not saying you don't have to work or exert effort to have or do what you want. Rather, when your actions are aligned with what matters to you, it won't *feel* as hard. Furthermore, simply throwing time and energy around to the point of exhaustion doesn't guarantee happiness or joy—in fact, it might just create more problems. If you aren't happy now, don't fall into the trap of believing that if you just work harder or do more, you will finally be happier. In my experience, doing more of what doesn't make you happy isn't how you get happier.

Instead, believe you can actually do less and be more. By focusing your energy on what matters and eliminating the noise, you can open space and time in your schedule while still achieving all you want to achieve. But note, I did say you have to cut the noise. You must be willing to let go of other people's shoulds and your own preconceptions of what success looks like. Your success will no longer be measured in hours worked or the "hardness" of the work done; it will be measured in meaningful (to you) output, whatever that may be. For me, it means measuring success in smiles. My goal is to spread joy and have joy, so when I have a day full of smiles—mine and other people's—it has been a good day.

Again, I am not saying that hard work doesn't have a place. It absolutely does. I am talking about the difference between focusing your energy and throwing it around. My daughter recently described this difference using a funnel analogy. "It's the difference between trying to fill a bottle from an open jar and using a funnel to fill it," she said. If you pour water over a bottle from a wide-lipped jar, you spill water everywhere—what a waste. But, if you use a funnel to direct the water from the jar into the bottle, you get a fuller bottle and less mess. My son likes his perspective of shooting a basketball. Standing at the free-throw line, you want to direct every muscle and all your physical energy toward putting the ball into the hoop. From toes to fingertips, everything is aligned and working toward a common goal. No matter which analogy you use, the concept is the same: you accomplish more—fill a bottle or score a basket—when you harness and focus your energy in a single direction. Alternatively, when you allow your energy to spread in a million different directions, you often just have a mess to clean up.

Meet Bill. A dreamer and an entrepreneur, Bill has big plans and works hard to achieve them. His biggest dream is to create a business-building education company teaching other entrepreneurs how to start successful companies. While he is working toward this goal, he's also working on two or three new company ideas. In any given week, he's splitting his time between planning content and classes for his business-building education company, selling product for other companies, reviewing contracts, hiring staff, interfacing with accountants and bankers, and doing everything else that comes with the day-to-day operations of a start-up. Is Bill doing anything wrong? Not exactly. But I can tell you this, Bill isn't happy. He's tired, overwhelmed, and concerned about whether he'll ever find time to build his dream company. Depending on Bill's nervous system, he's either shut down already or is indiscriminately trying to do it all while slowly driving himself to the point of exhaustion at which he'll have no choice but to shut down.

Put another way, Bill is trying to build a village; but instead of focusing on one house and one brick at a time, he's adding fragments of brick to several houses and then feeling discouraged and overwhelmed when he doesn't see structures taking shape. In reality, he can build all the houses he wants—but I think we can all agree that it will be more efficient, more fulfilling, and frankly easier if Bill focuses his energy on one house at a time and one brick at a time within that house. To be clear, I am not saying that Bill can only build his business-building education company and must shutter all the other companies. Nor am I saying that Bill can resolve this tension overnight.

What I am suggesting is that Bill prioritize his most important house right now and focus on adding complete bricks to that house. In addition, Bill can identify the relative priority of the bricks of the other houses—focusing on the bricks most important to their structure and then meaningfully and effectively working on these houses when he has time, or working to identify additional resources necessary to their construction. That said, Bill could also choose to put his entire focus into the construction of his dream house.

At the end of the day, it is simply about choosing to be mindful of how you spend your energy and recognizing that concentrated energy can accomplish more with less. Reality check: I recognize that sometimes we don't have the flexibility to choose how we spend all of our energy. Simply realizing those limitations can be useful. Understanding what portion of your capacity (time, energy, and resources) you can direct and then focusing it on what matters can powerfully impact your happiness.

To unwind this barrier belief, you may need to undo years of programming. While you might want freedom and space in your schedule for adventure and fun, you might also believe that you must be working every available hour because hard work is what generates abundance. As you focus more on what you want and eliminate what exhausts and overwhelms you, you may feel like you aren't working hard enough and, therefore, can't have or don't deserve the happiness you are experiencing. You will suddenly have room in your schedule or space in your brain that you didn't have before. Your initial instinct will probably be to fill this space with something. You may feel a pull to add more to your plate because, after all, working more means having more. This is your belief—incompatible with your desire—that is pulling you back into the Emotional Energy Gap. Below, I suggest alternatives that might give you greater appreciation for your newfound spaciousness. I am asking you to make a potentially radical mind shift. I am asking you to believe something that you've probably never been taught and maybe never experienced.

As you move closer to living a life aligned with your priorities, you will find more space for the things you want to do. You will find more space in your life because you have made that space nonnegotiable. That space isn't there to be filled with mindless energy expenditure so that you can prove that you are working hard enough to earn happiness. As we move forward on this journey, I want you to commit fully to creating space in your life for the things that matter to you. You need to be committed to measuring your output not by the hours you put in, but the quality and satisfaction you get out. To understand where your satisfaction comes from, the next activity asks you to get clear on what actually brings you joy—and what doesn't.

ACTION STEP:
SOURCE JOY

To know where to put your energy, let's begin with what brings you joy already (or happiness or contentment or fun). Start by journaling for five to ten minutes on the following prompts. As we've discussed, your journaling can take a form that works for you: typing, handwriting, recording a voice memo, or talking with a friend. Just find some way to memorialize what you learn so you can reflect back on it.

Prompt One: I feel joyful (or happy) when . . .

As you think about this prompt, consider times in your life or recent memory when you've been really happy. Ask yourself the following questions:

What is it about that thing or time that was joyful?

Dig deep and list all the aspects of that thing or experience that brought you joy. For example, if being on a beach vacation brings you joy is it the fact that you don't have to work, exploring a new place, or just being near the water. Try to distill the sources of your joy to their essence.

Prompt Two: What did I tell yourself about whether I deserved that happiness?

Did I earn it somehow?

What did others tell me about whether I deserved that happiness?

When I use this exercise with clients, they either ascribe their happiness to bone-crushing effort to the exclusion of all else *or* luck. Rarely do I meet a client who answers with something like: "I worked hard on this project or thing because it really mattered to me, I had fun doing it and I am so proud of the result."

I also want to take a moment here to ask you to think about the difference between comfort and happiness or joy. Often, when we are in a comfortable space, we can mistake that feeling for joy or happiness. That is our nervous system trying to keep us safe. I want to remind you that often joy and happiness can be found at the edge or even outside our comfort zone.

Prompt Three: Some things that I do (with my time, energy, or resources) that don't bring me joy are . . .

Knowing what these things are is equally important. Does hard work bring you joy? Does hustle bring you joy? Does an overflowing to-do list bring you joy? As with your sources of joy, try to really understand the root of what is not joyful for you about these things. Ultimately, the goal of this exercise is to understand what drives happiness for you so that you can begin to do more of those things. It may also highlight where you are stuck in old patterns around what you think you need to do to achieve happiness.

This journaling activity is not an exercise that will immediately result in changed behavior. Rather, it will deepen your understanding of your relationship with hard work and hustle. And perhaps it will invite you to explore the idea that joy can come freely—no strings attached—when you align with what matters to you.

When you engage a more priority-aligned lifestyle, you are engaging a life where you spend time on what matters to you—not one where you ineffectively throw time at the problem of your unhappiness. How many times have you been told or told someone else: "If you just worked harder, then you would . . . ?" I've raised teenagers—this isn't about those times when working harder is actually the remedy (e.g., "Mom, I wish I'd earned a better grade on this test I didn't really study for"). This is about those times when we fall victim to the idea that if we just tried harder and did more, we'd be happier. In his book, *Essentialism*, Greg McKeown says it like this:

> What if society stopped telling us to buy more
> stuff and instead allowed us to create more
> space to breathe and think? What if society
> encouraged us to reject what has been accu-

rately described as doing things we detest,
to buy things we don't need, with money we
don't have, to impress people we don't like?

I encourage you to suspend any ideas about the effort required for happiness. Instead, consider that happiness is born out of having time and space to spend your energy in the ways and on the things most important to you. And that might mean you are happy without having to pay for joy with suffering.

Ultimately, your happiness is your birthright. You are allowed to be happy. There is no magic formula for earning happiness. No set number of hours you must work to be rewarded with joy. Instead, your happiness rests solely in your control. It's yours for the taking. Yours for the savoring. And, like the waves in the sea and the wind in the sky, it doesn't need to be pushed—you can just let it flow.

Chapter 10

BREAKTHROUGH BEHAVIOR #3 CLAIMING CONTROL

Next, I want to talk about some of the barrier beliefs you might have about choice. Too often, when discussing a needed change, we respond with something like, "But I don't have a choice." Sometimes this is true, but more often we have not claimed our control. Claiming your control comes down to the power of choice.

I'd like to tell you the story of my firstborn, my daughter, at the willful age of ten. On many days, she'd find herself deadlocked in an argument with her younger brother, then six, because he refused to play the game (it could be Barbies, a board game, or a make-believe game) the way she thought it should be played. This argument would escalate. Her little brother would raise his voice; she would raise hers. Sometimes he'd throw something or lash out. And sometimes she'd do it back. When it got loud enough or generated tears, a parent would be summoned. This little girl would be resolutely focused on the fairness of the situation—it was *not fair* that little brother didn't play by the rules, it was *not fair* that he hit her first, it was *not fair* that he yelled so loud, and it was *not fair* that he said mean things. Every time I was the summoned parent, I would respond to her entreaties by asking: "What can you control in this situation?" Sometimes the answer came quickly, sometimes it required longer conversation, but always it was the same. "I can control myself." Over time, this conversation evolved to include a second question: "Did you behave in a way you are proud of?" And, as this conversation turned from interactions with her brother to managing social interactions in middle and high school: "How can you handle it in a way you will be proud of?"

I am not a parenting genius. This didn't work perfectly or prevent my daughter from ever making the wrong choice. But it gave her a framework for approaching challenging situations in a way that allows her to direct her energy toward what matters, instead of getting hung up on things she can't control. She's learned that, by asking these questions in an emotionally charged situation, she can shift her perspective back to what really matters. Recognizing that she can choose her perspective is also essential to this process.

Many things vie to constrain our personal choice—we live in a society with systemic limitations, laws, and very real obligations. While many aspects of life are outside our control, we often fail to recognize the amount of influence we have on our happiness by claiming control of our thoughts, feelings, perspective, and actions. In any given situation, you can choose what you think about it, how you feel about it, and what you will do about it (including nothing). In addition, you can choose responses that you can be proud of; or, said another way, you can make sure your responses are aligned with your priorities.

Meet Sarah. She is a CEO growing her company. We had spent our most recent coaching session identifying her top three areas of professional focus for the coming weeks. She was certain these three things, mostly centered around hiring, had to get done, were the most important to the growth of her company and would require her time. I then asked her a question I often ask my clients: "When will you block time on your calendar to get these three things done?" She opened her calendar and explained that she couldn't make any time in the next three days because she *had* to attend back-to-back meetings about project X—a totally different initiative. In this moment, I realized this session—like many others—had gotten to the most important issue right at the end. She hadn't yet recognized that she had the power of choice. I asked her, "Is project X more important than hiring?" She responded, "No." So I asked, "What can you do to reflect that hiring is more important in how you spend your time this week?" After much equivocating on her part—explaining why if she postponed or didn't attend the project X meetings, someone would be disappointed or mad—I finally asked, "You're the CEO, right? I recognize this is a slight simplification, but what do you really *have* to do besides sleep, eat, and breathe? Everything else is a choice—what do you want to choose here?" After a brief silence, she acknowledged that while project X was important, hiring was more important. She would go to the executive in charge of project X and explain why she needed to reclaim her time this week, and they'd determine together which meetings could either be postponed or missed. Moreover, as we continued our work together, Sarah began to embrace the notion that just because she *can*—she's capable, able, or knowledgeable— doesn't mean she *should*. She realized that she had control over how she chose to spend her energy and when she chose to delegate.

ACTION STEP:
MULTIPLE CHOICE

Here, you'll get realistic about your level of control over your life choices. Think about a situation that you are currently struggling with and journal for five minutes (yes, exactly five minutes) on the following prompts:

In this situation, I can control . . .

With what feels out of my control, is it really that I dislike the trade-offs I am being asked to make?

If I had to make a choice between those trade-offs, what would my priorities tell me to choose?

If that choice feels uncomfortable to me, why is that?

Have I considered just doing nothing?

Your life might be a little different than Sarah's. You might not be the CEO of your company. But you do have choices. And yes, choices come with consequences and trade-offs. A choice to spend more time with your family may mean you forgo a professional opportunity. That choice may have an impact on your wallet. That only matters if it matters to you. And it should only influence your choice if the loss is more important—or a higher priority—than the gain.

You may not always be able to choose what matters to you most. For example, if you get called to jury duty, I'm not suggesting you shirk your civic duty. You probably should show up even if it means time away from your top priority. But you can appreciate that you are choosing to show up for jury duty because civic duty matters and the consequences for not showing up are not worth it to you. Recognizing that nearly everything you do is a choice is central to leading a more priority-aligned life.

If you find yourself struggling to choose between competing priorities, don't worry. We will dive deeper into prioritizing the pieces of your life in part III. But perhaps you are already recognizing that you have more than one important thing and you don't know how to choose—either because all the choices feel wrong or too many of them feel right. It is unrealistic to expect that one book will bring you complete clarity on all your choices. Remember, this is a process. This is a balance dance. The dance starts with understanding what really matters to you. Then it moves to recognizing the tensions that can arise between those things. Knowing that this tension is a potential source of unhappiness, you may need to test different approaches.

If you get really stuck between two competing priorities, that is an excellent time to enlist outside support. This could be a friend, a colleague, a partner, or even a professional like a therapist or coach. Sometimes lingering tension between priorities comes from a failure to really be honest about the season you are in, and sometimes it's about still being under the shadow of other people's shoulds. Whatever the source for you, I encourage you to recognize the tension is there and ask for help. Bottom line: know that you have more control than you have claimed around how, when, and where you spend your time, energy, and resources. It's time to recognize that and start using it to architect a happier life.

Chapter 11

BREAKTHROUGH BEHAVIOR #4
ALL THE FEELINGS

Often people think that to live a happier life, they should just ignore or minimize the bad or difficult feelings. To me, having joy ultimately requires feeling all the feelings. If you only engage with happy and uplifting emotions, you can't get all the way to joy. As you make the changes needed to live a happier, priority-aligned life, you will need to confront some uncomfortable feelings. You might find this easy, but you might also find that you are not accustomed to sitting with your discomfort. As a society, we are sent message after message that uncomfortable feelings are to be avoided or numbed. I am here to tell you that uncomfortable feelings are to be felt. Let me say it again: you need your uncomfortable feelings like fear, anger, sadness, disappointment, guilt, and boredom just as much as you need gratitude, happiness, love, and joy. Your uncomfortable feelings are the ones that tell you when you need to make a change, where you need to grow, or that you are growing.

Ultimately, you can't have the happiness and joy you seek if you avoid working through discomfort when it arises. If you dismiss an uncomfortable feeling without addressing it, you've only delayed and probably expanded it. While it can be new, different, and even outright difficult to sit with and listen to your uncomfortable feelings, I highly recommend doing so because every feeling brings wisdom—every single feeling has a message. And when you don't listen, feelings—especially the difficult ones—tend to act like a petulant toddler getting louder and louder until you are forced to hear their message. If this is a new process for you, giving your uncomfortable feelings space may feel like sitting down for coffee with an unwelcome stranger. And, in fact, that is a good way to think of it. Think of it as a coffee meeting, where your only job is to listen and ask questions. You don't have to stay at the coffee shop forever, but you do need to finish the conversation. And if going to this meeting alone is too hard, invite a friend.

I want to share a technique I use to manage uncomfortable emotions. Whether you use this exercise now or tuck it in your toolbox for later, familiarize yourself with this practice now. With a basic understanding, you can easily implement it on the fly. And, like any muscle, the more you exercise your coping-with-uncomfortable-feelings muscle, the easier it will get.

As I mentioned, I'm married to a basketball coach and I'm raising two basketball players. I've watched a lot of basketball over the last five years. A lot. I also like to keep the book. (I've always had a thing for filling out forms.) There are two kinds of time-outs in basketball: the longer is a minute and thirty seconds, and the shorter is just thirty seconds. During many games spent at the scorer's table, I've observed that these two time-outs serve different purposes. The longer time-out is typically used when players need a rest or when the coach needs to communicate a more detailed message about strategy or game play—for example, a new play. The 30-second time-out is reserved for situations when a reset is needed—when the players have lost track of what they are supposed to be doing, when the momentum of the game needs to be shifted, or when the game appears to be getting out of control.

This action step can serve the same role as the latter. It can be employed in those moments when your emotions start to overtake your logic. You can take a 30-second time-out and work through what you are feeling and quickly move past it.

ACTION STEP:
THE 30-SECOND TIME-OUT

This activity asks you to explore your uncomfortable feeling, then thank it and release it. If this sounds awful and hard already, bear with me. Disclaimer: when I talk about uncomfortable feelings, I am talking about manageable uncomfortable feelings. This exercise is not a comprehensive solution for managing the discomfort that might come with trauma, anxiety, depression, or any other mental health response. When exploring manageable uncomfortable feelings, I am suggesting you engage with your discomfort, but do not stay there. Don't bite off more than you can chew. I trust you to know your emotional health and what you can and can't do without additional support. If you need additional support to manage your feelings, please don't hesitate to get it.

This exercise also asks you to lead with curiosity, not judgment. As you explore your uncomfortable feelings, you may find yourself wanting to get judgmental. You may have a feeling—like fear—and you may start with the self-talk that sounds like encouragement but is really judgment. Self-talk like: *Come on, you can do this. You are being silly. Why are you always afraid? Just suck it up and do it.* Please refrain from that sort of self-talk, at least for the duration of this exercise. I want you, to get curious. Instead of telling your feelings to go away or telling yourself what to do, only ask questions. Seek to understand why that feeling is here and what it is trying to show or tell you—and whether that message is true for you.

Consider an uncomfortable feeling you are having right now and answer the following questions:

What am I feeling?

Sometimes this answer will be obvious. I encourage you to sit with your feeling a bit longer than you normally would—you may find there is more to it than you thought. For example, in the quiet space you create, your anger might reveal itself to be fear or sadness. I encourage you to go beyond simply naming your feeling (e.g., "I'm angry"). Instead, explain in one or two sentences what you think the source of your feeling is. For example, "I am feeling scared that if I start to say no to people, they won't be willing to say yes to me."

Where am I feeling it?

Name where in your body you are feeling this. As we discussed in chapter 6, a lot of information is communicated from the body to the brain. This is a great opportunity to hone your understanding of your Indicator Light. Understanding your physical cues for uncomfortable feelings can be helpful in managing them because we often feel in our bodies before we register the feeling with our minds.

What can I learn from it—what wisdom is it trying to share? Is that wisdom true?

Here, think about what this feeling is really trying to tell you. Then evaluate whether that wisdom fits the facts or only fits the past. For example, if I am afraid that if I start saying no, others won't say yes, I might initially perceive that the wisdom is: "Don't say no." That might be wisdom my body and brain gleaned from childhood, when I was told that what my parents said was the law and that I couldn't say no to their requests. That wisdom does not fit my current facts as an adult—it's based in the past. Instead, this feeling might be telling my adult self that I care deeply about my friendships and relationships and that although I'm committed to choosing what I need, I want to do so in a way that is respectful of the extent of that caring.

How can I thank and release it?

Staying in discomfort isn't the solution. Once you've gotten the message from the uncomfortable feeling, it's time to let it go. Consider how you might thank it and release it. It might be enough to simply say something like: "Thank you, fear, for reminding me that I care deeply about the people in my life. I understand your message and will keep it in mind as I make this change." For other feelings, the release process may require more time, more thought, or even

conversation with other people. Explore what comes up for
you, then trust your intuition and do it.

I recently used this exercise with a friend. She was struggling to make holiday plans and was feeling stuck. She and her family really wanted to stay home for the Thanksgiving holiday. Her parents and siblings wanted her to come back to her childhood home—a cross-country flight away. It had been a crazy year—she was exhausted and so were her kids. The last thing she wanted was to pack them up and get on a plane during the busiest travel season. But she felt bad. She felt guilty. And when she thought about traveling to her family, she also felt resentful. They didn't seem to understand how exhausted she was. She didn't know how to resolve those feelings and make a decision.

Together we walked through the questions in the action step above. She described three feelings: guilt about not doing what she should and going to see her family, sadness about her aging parents missing the opportunity to see her kids, and frustration that her family didn't seem to understand how hard she'd been working. She felt these feelings in her gut and her throat. Finally, I asked her what these feelings might be telling her. The sadness was easy—it was telling her that she loved her parents, she knew that they were getting older and that it mattered to her that her kids have time with them. But, she quickly recognized, it didn't have to be this particular time.

Guilt was a little more complicated. That went back to a broader need to do the right thing. After further conversation, she was committed to defining *her* right thing instead of being stuck with someone else's—and in this case, the right thing for her and for her immediate family was not to travel on this particular holiday. Finally, she realized her frustration was telling her that she wanted her family to know how hard it had recently been and how much she was struggling. We thanked her feelings for their clarity and insight and we moved on to other topics—probably reality TV.

A couple of days later, she reached out to her parents in California and had a heart-to-heart about just how over-whelmed she'd been. Because they loved her and knew what a hard-charging personality she was, they suggested that she take the Thanksgiving holiday as a break and stay local. Together they planned to FaceTime during their respective dinners so they could still connect as a family. And they put a tentative future visit on the calendar when both she and the kids would have more time. She was relieved, she got some much-needed downtime, and nobody got hurt.

In some circumstances, releasing your feelings might require more time, reflection, or support. For bigger issues, I've used coaching, meditation, energy work, and therapy. Be patient with yourself. If you've been avoiding this feeling for some time, it might keep popping up and take several efforts to finally feel like you can release it. Explore what feels right for you. Also, because navigating difficult feelings is a process and growth is not linear, continue using this exercise through-out the rest of the book and any time you encounter a difficult emotion. This framework is great for almost anyone in any sit-uation at any age. You can also use this exercise with the awe-some emotions—it can be fun to explicitly give them a chance to share their messages, too.

Making the change to living a priority-aligned life is a big deal. And as a result, it comes with big feelings. Feeling all the feelings allows you to work through the emotions that arise as you authentically claim what you want and need. It also allows you to manage the feelings that might come up as you start to live your priorities—matching your time to what matters most to you (not anyone else).

Chapter 12

BREAKTHROUGH BEHAVIOR #5 RELEASING GUILT

As we learn to manage uncomfortable feelings on the path to living a happier, more priority-aligned life, we need to talk about one feeling in particular—guilt. I suspect guilt will come up as you shift your focus from what is currently filling your time and taking your energy to the things that matter to you. This common barrier belief sounds like: "If I feel guilty, that means I shouldn't do it." If you've been feeling that guilty tug, know that it is normal and that you can overcome it.

The first step to overcoming your guilt is understanding its source. Healthy guilt comes up when we have violated our own moral standards or the rules and morals of our community. For example, it is normal and appropriate to feel guilty when we lie or break the law. That guilt is telling us to not break rules and to make amends if we have. However, things get muddled when we feel guilt for what we perceive as a violation of the rules or values of a particular person or community (e.g., past self, family, social group) without first considering whether we share those values or not.

Let me say it another way: guilt is sometimes code for "I am afraid that I will let my community down or be judged by my community if I do or don't do something." Framed this way, here's how you can move through this type of guilt: confirm that your community's values are what you think they are and then assess whether those values match your own. If you discover your values match, guilt is probably appropriately telling you to change your behavior. If your values aren't aligned, you don't need to let guilt about violating values that you don't hold determine your actions.

Let me make this more concrete. I have told you that my mother put her career first. What I have not explicitly said is that she went to law school after she had had a child (me), in the late seventies and early eighties (a time when there weren't many women in law). This is just one of the many reasons that I view her as a professional trailblazer. As mentioned, I reached a time in my professional life when I wanted to put being a parent first. What I have not told you is the level of guilt I grappled with in making this decision. I felt guilty that I'd spent time and resources—mine and my parents—pursuing an educational path that I was considering not using, or at least not using in the expected way. This guilt assumed that I wouldn't benefit from and use my legal education in my future endeavors, because I wouldn't be a practicing lawyer. I felt guilty that I wasn't continuing on the trail of professional achievement that my mom had blazed. I assumed she felt that prioritizing career was important, and that in her eyes, my success should be measured by my professional achievements. I felt guilty that I hadn't been giving enough attention to my then two-year-old and wondered whether I'd be making this shift too late. I assumed that I'd done irreparable damage with my absence.

I can remember the fear I felt as I told my parents I was going to make a significant professional change and prioritize motherhood. I was afraid of the disappointment I just knew I would hear in my mother's voice. With a pounding heart, I picked up the phone to have that conversation. I knew I needed to claim my priorities. I was determined to make this change in my life, despite all the guilt I was feeling. But I also knew I needed to confront this guilt, because it was heavy.

What I found on the other end of the phone was nothing but complete acceptance. You see, I'd gotten it twisted. My community (family) didn't value professional success above all else; my family valued living your priorities. They were happy to honor—even celebrate—that I had identified what mattered to me and was taking steps to align with my priorities. Of course the person who had so influentially demonstrated the power of living a priority-aligned life would support my efforts to do the same. But I was so caught up in what I thought mattered to my family, I had forgotten to actually consider whether my assumptions were right. I failed to understand what my community actually valued.

As you'll recall, my choice to be a mom first didn't mean that I decided to be a stay-at-home parent. Instead, I recognized that to be the best parent I could be, I needed a place to engage and challenge my brain outside of parenting. Being a mom first meant that when confronted with situations where I was asked to choose between my job and my kids, I was going to choose my kids as often as possible. Because I chose this path, I also had (and still sometimes have) mom guilt. There are times when I see what other parents do and wonder whether I am doing enough. There are also times when I have felt judged by other parents for choosing to have a job outside the home.

To manage this guilt, I need to be completely secure in two things. First, to be a good mom (and human), I have to do work outside of parenting. For me, that is a fact, not a choice. That someone else is able to make another choice and be happy is no reason for me to feel bad about my facts. Second, I know that, more often than not, I show up for my family when it matters. I'm not perfect, but I am good enough. I know that because we talk about it. Because my community (my family) and I are on the same page, it is way easier to care a lot less about the decisions people outside my family have chosen. In other words, the only community values that matter to me on this issue are those of my immediate family.

ACTION STEP:
UNPACKING GUILT

If feelings of guilt are popping up as you move toward doing less and being more, I encourage you to explore them. This exploration is critically important if the guilt is blocking you from moving forward. It can also be meaningful if the guilt isn't stopping you but instead you are carrying it as you move forward. Dropping that guilt burden is one way to lighten your load.

Step One: Describe your guilt.

You can use the following format to make a statement about your guilt. "I feel guilty because . . ." Your statement might sound something like: "I feel guilty because I am choosing to spend time on self-care instead of going to a party."

Step Two: Dig a little deeper.

Take what you put in that blank and ask yourself: *Where is this coming from?* and *Why do I believe this to be true?* This might look something like: "I believe if I don't go to the party, my friends will be mad at me and I will miss out on something fun."

Step Three: Dig even deeper.

Take your answers from the question above and ask yourself: *Why do I care?* The answer might be something like: "I care because I want my friends to like and accept me." About now, your rational, calm brain might be showing up to say chime in with some wisdom along the lines of: "Silly rabbit, you know your friends love you and they won't reject you for needing to take time for yourself. And besides, if they do, are those the friends you really want?" If this is where you land, you've identified a values mismatch that is really underlying your guilt. In friendship, you value authenticity. So if your friends can't accept your doing what you have decided you need, they aren't the friends you want. Buh-bye guilt. You can stop here, but you can also keep going.

Step Four: Dig all the way to the root.

Take your step three answer, and ask: *Why am I afraid of this?* The answer might be something like: "I am afraid that I'm not really that likable, and if I stop showing up to things, I won't just miss out on fun, I also won't be missed. I am afraid I'm not good enough." When you get to this place, you've identified the true source of your guilt. You may need to ask this question more than once to get to the root and your fear. Give yourself permission to ask it as many times as it takes.

Step Five: Turn it around.

When you've identified the root belief, it's time to identify the opposite. Write a statement that is the opposite of your root belief that you also believe could be true. For some this might look something like: "I am awesome, and my friends know it. I don't need to worry about not being good enough." For others, it might simply be: "I believe my friends can understand that I have needs and that it is okay for me to take care of myself."

This exercise should help you figure out whether you want to hold on to or let go of the guilt you are carrying. Know that if you are used to carrying a lot of guilt, letting go will feel weird—and may even make you feel a little guilty. But keep running through these questions—the more you do, the easier it gets. I am not promising you a guilt-free life. Remember, guilt is appropriate when you have crossed a line that matters to you. Ultimately, guilt can be a feeling with purpose and value, so it is a good idea to check in and listen to its messages. For example, if I am feeling guilty for choosing self-care over my friends, in part because I am worried that I've hurt their feelings, I can let my friends know that they matter to me. I can reach out and let them know that while I prioritized my self-care over this particular get-together, they do matter to me and I am sorry if that choice (which I stand by) hurt their feelings. Guilt, in its best moments, can be a powerful reminder of just how much we care about other people.

Chapter 13

BREAKTHROUGH BEHAVIOR #6
SAY NO

Priority-aligned living asks you to say no to what doesn't matter to you and your happiness. On the surface, that sounds easy enough, but in practice, it can be hard and feel uncomfortable. If you are not used to saying no or are a self-identified people pleaser and just the thought of saying no is making you feel slightly nauseated, take heart. I will guide you through the process of saying no. I am not promising it will be easy right away—but I know you can do it. While saying no is one of the biggest places of discomfort for people along the path to priority-aligned living, it is a powerful way to move toward your happiness.

To remove the noise from your life—the things that take your energy, time, and resources but aren't important to you—you will need to say no. You may find you need to say no a lot. Earlier, I asked you to get comfortable with the idea of saying no, now I'm going to give you some practical and empowering tips to actually do it. Remember, it is okay if saying no is new or uncomfortable to you. That is normal. And, if you've already gotten this far, you've proven that you can do uncomfortable things when they matter to you.

Let's talk about why saying no might be hard. It might be hard because you haven't had much practice, but in my experience, there's usually something deeper. For many people, saying no brings up beliefs and feelings that are inconsistent with saying no. Common ones I've seen come up are: "My needs aren't *that* important," "It's just nicer to say yes," "I am afraid that I won't be liked if I say no," or "I'm afraid of missing out." If saying no is connected to an old belief or feeling for you, it is helpful to identify it. If you are struggling to identify it, consider the particular situation in which you would like to say no and ask yourself what you would need to believe or feel about yourself or the situation in order to say no. Often this exercise alone will be enough to get you unstuck.

For example, I worked with a client, Beth, who was routinely presented with investment opportunities. As a self-identified people pleaser, Beth struggled to say no when friends brought opportunities to her. She loved investing with her friends, but only when those investments were a good fit for her overall investing strategy. In a coaching session, I asked her what she would need to believe about herself or the situation if she said no to some of these investment opportunities. It took her a while to explore this answer. It started with things like, "I'd have to believe that my friends don't like me just for my money" (true, but not the real issue), and "I'd have to believe that people won't hate me if I don't give them money" (also true, but not really the root). Finally, with a laugh, she said something like, "I'd have to believe that I get to say what I do with my hard-earned money and nobody gets to judge me for it." That was the belief that unlocked her ability to say no. She realized she could explain to her friends that she had a particular investment strategy for her portfolio and that their investment didn't meet her needs. She could tell them she was excited for them and the possibility of their success, but that she didn't want to or couldn't put her money there. I'd be lying if I said that saying no was easy for her after this conversation, it wasn't. But it was easier.

Once you feel or believe you are empowered to say no, these tips make saying no as painless as possible: be clear, be honest, be quick, and be kind. I know these tips because I used to break *every single one.* For example, I've been known to respond to invitations to friend's parties by sending a text or email like the one below. A communication sent the day before the party that I wasn't attending because I was exhausted and just needed a night to myself: "OMG, I am so sorry this response is so late. I don't think I can make your party—I've got a work thing. If I happen to finish up sooner, I will swing by. XOXO."

This kind of message, which was not uncommon for me in my twenties and thirties, broke all the rules. Let's take them one by one.

When you need to tell someone no, be clear with yourself on why you are saying no and be clear with the other person that you are saying no. Part of your internal clarity will come from your supporting beliefs and feelings. It may also come from living a priority-aligned life and knowing what you are being asked to do or give doesn't align with your current priorities. For example, in the message above, I said I had a work thing, but the truth was that I was prioritizing self-care over this social event. My own lack of clarity prevented me from being clear with my friends, being honest, being timely, and being kind. Thankfully, I now have a much better understanding of what matters to me and am more equipped to articulate it to myself and the people around me.

My message didn't clearly express that I wouldn't be attending the party. I said, "I don't think I can make your party

. . . [but I might] swing by," instead of just saying I wouldn't be there. When we are feeling nervous about hurting someone's feelings or being judged, we too often equivocate. We try to soften the blow, and in doing so, we muddy the waters. We leave the receiver of our message unclear as to whether we are saying no or whether we are saying maybe. To avoid this, ensure you are leading with clear language that you don't later undo or confuse. If you are writing an email or text to say no, the words *no, can't,* or *won't* would probably be included. By giving the impression that I might show up at my friend's party, I was saying maybe when I meant no.

My message wasn't honest. To avoid hurt or judgment, we often make excuses that are sometimes flat-out lies. In my example above, I didn't have a work commitment—I wanted (or needed) to prioritize self-care, but I didn't feel empowered to say so. An honest no doesn't have to include information you don't want to share, but it shouldn't include information that is patently false. So instead of the lie above, you could simply say, "I can't come to the party." Or if you feel comfortable sharing more you could say, "I'm exhausted and need to stay home tonight, so I'm not going to make it to your party."

When you are saying no, don't delay. I still struggle the most with this one. I don't like to let people down, so sometimes I don't answer and hope they will forget they asked. This isn't the right approach and it isn't fair. If you can't or won't do something and you know it, say so. Don't create false hope by delaying. Don't make someone follow up on a request you know is a no. And if you really don't know until the last minute, just do the right thing and say no when you know.

Finally, be kind. You can remind the receiver that you care. Or even offer an alternative if you want to. *No* doesn't have to be all business and no love. But only offer an alternative if you mean it. Putting it all together, I could have said something like: "I apologize for the last-minute notice; I can't make it to your party. I really appreciate your reaching out to include me, and I hope you have a great time. I can't wait to see all the pictures from the fun on your Insta. I do miss you, and I'd love to have coffee next week if you have time—would Tuesday work?"

But don't say any of that if it's not important to you or not true. Don't offer an alternative to equivocate or soften the blow if you have no intention of acting on it. You could cut your no off after the first two sentences if you don't care about the pictures on the social channels or you don't want to prioritize time with your friend later. Recognize that when you start to approach saying no this way, it will feel unfamiliar. Notice when you want to equivocate or when you are uncomfortable with saying no and consider what that feeling is trying to tell you. Work through your feelings—using the exercise in chapter 11 if you need additional support. Feeling uncomfortable is not a reason to avoid saying no. Saying no is the biggest game changer. Get good at it, and it will be good to you.

ACTION STEP:
LEARN YOUR *NO* PATTERNS

Rather than thinking about a looming no, let's look at a previous time you said no and it didn't go so well. Consider:

Were you clear? If not, how could you have gotten or been clearer?

Were you honest? If not, how could you have said it differently?

Were you quick? Did you say no as soon as you knew? If not, when should you have said no?

Were you kind? If not, how could you have phrased it differently?

Playing Monday-morning quarterback, it is always easier to see the right plays after the fact than when you're on-field in the pressure situation. By evaluating times you've said no in the past, you can familiarize yourself with your patterns around saying no. You will notice if you tend to delay or equivocate. You will notice if you throw in little lies to soften the blow. And if you do all these things—it's cool. You're just like me. Which means I know you can change these things—because I have.

Remember, saying no is a gift. It's a gift to you—because it enables you to preserve your time, energy, and resources for things that matter most to you. And when done clearly, honestly, quickly, and kindly, it is a gift to someone else. It helps them understand exactly what to expect and removes confusion about your intentions. Saying no is a muscle worth training if you want to close your Physical Energy Gap and focus your time, energy, and resources on what matters to you. Being vocal and honest about your priorities also helps you close the Authenticity Gap. One last thought: because saying no is a gift, when someone tells you no—and especially if they do it clearly, honestly, quickly, and kindly—you might consider thanking them.

Chapter 14

BREAKTHROUGH BEHAVIOR #7
MAGIC MANTRAS

In the next two chapters, you'll learn two no-fail solutions to employ when nothing else is working to shift your beliefs and feelings and close the Emotional Energy Gap: mantras and support. If you had told me a decade ago I'd be writing a book in which I call mantras "magic," I would have laughed in your face. In part, that's because I wasn't yet honest with myself about the depth of my spiritual openness, but in part it's because I hadn't experienced their power myself. If you are thinking, *No ma'am, no mantras for me,* that's cool. But I encourage you to open your mind enough to consider adding mantras to your toolbox—a time might come when you've tried everything else and it is the only thing that works.

Sometimes when you are trying to change your behavior, old feelings stand in the way. For example, I have never thought of myself as an athlete. I walked the half mile in middle school. I walked during soccer warm-ups. Even as an adult,

I found myself quitting a workout whenever it felt "too hard." I've struggled with my weight and fitness for as long as I can remember. I've tried all sorts of things to change it: I've done diets, hired a functional medicine coach, joined Beachbody, joined gyms, tried a million different workouts, learned about the science of habits, and so much more. Let me be clear, there is nothing wrong with any of these tools—they are all useful, I still use some of them, and for many people, they are just what is needed. The problem was, when it came to doing hard things with my body, I already had the only tool I needed, I just wasn't using it.

My breakthrough came during the COVID-19 quarantine. My family of four started walking in our not-so-flat neighborhood together. I loved our walks. But I didn't love that every time we got to the steepest hills and my husband and children bounded ahead of me, my mind convinced me that my body wanted to quit. Let me say it this way: my body (although not super fit) was fine, strong, and capable, but my mind kept telling me it was time to stop, that I was falling behind and I should just quit. Or so I thought. The more I educated myself on the role of the nervous system, the more I realized that it wasn't exactly my mind telling me to quit, it was my nervous system telling my brain to quit. Once I made that connection, I spent several walks figuring out where that message was really coming from. Then I remembered a story my mother told me about my childhood, something I had completely forgotten. In the late years of elementary school, I lived abroad. When we'd run outside for gym, the teacher would follow behind, and if you ran too slow, he'd hold a pencil between your shoulder blades to "encourage" you to run faster. My shoulders and that pencil were intimately acquainted. It made me miserable and I complained mightily about it (who wouldn't?!), reported my mom.

Fast-forward to January of my seventh-grade year, when we moved back to the United States and I was soon expected to run the mile for gym class. I can remember being absolutely terrified. First, I was convinced I couldn't do it—I'd gained a substantial amount of weight in the short time we had been home, which made running the mile even harder. Second, I knew I needed to do it, and under the time limit, to pass gym. Third, I was struggling mightily to fit into a new school, and running that mile felt like belonging. When it came time to run the mile, I walked most of it. I was by far the last to finish. My entire gym class and teachers were waiting at the finish line, as I ran the last two hundred yards while shame burned through every single cell in my body. In fact, I can still picture it in my mind's eye and feel it in my gut today. I am pretty sure my teachers and classmates were encouraging me—but that didn't matter. Shame overcame any positive emotion I might have had.

As my adult self processed these memories, I realized why, when I was falling behind my family, my nervous system suggested I stop. It was trying to keep me safe from that shame. The shame of being left behind. The shame of being last. The shame of being unfit. This realization was a game changer.

The tool I needed was simply my nervous system. I needed to get it on board with the idea that when I'm out walking with my family and falling behind or when I'm doing a hard workout, I don't have to fear shame. More importantly, I needed my nervous system to realize that, despite what it thinks, I'm safe. So, I came up with a mantra. I thought about what I would need to *believe* (at a nervous system level), what I would need to *feel*, and what I would need to *do* to change the pattern. When I was out walking and experienced the "I should quit" feeling—I usually noticed it immediately in my gut but sometimes didn't catch it until I'd stopped walking—I would repeat to myself, along with each step or each breath: "I am safe. I am strong. I can do this." It was magic. Within days, I was past the point of stopping; and within weeks, I found myself walking over three miles daily with no hesitation. I'm sure some readers are thinking: *Three miles. So what? That's no big deal.* But it's not the distance or the activity that matters, it's that using this simple mantra allowed me to move from quitting to finishing. The mantra was the one small thing that changed everything—the thing I needed to get past that old feeling of discomfort and shame standing between me and enjoying physical activity.

ACTION STEP:
REFRAMING MANTRA

If you are stalled in adopting a new habit or behavior, and think you might be stuck in an old feeling or belief, consider these questions:

What is the opposite of what you are struggling with (the opposite of the trigger or old feeling)?

What do you need to feel or believe about yourself to do that thing?

What outcome do you want?

Then put those answers together to generate a mantra using this simple formula:

> *Opposite + belief or feeling + outcome = Mantra*
>
> For me it was: "I am safe," the opposite of what my nervous system was telling my brain; "I am strong," what I needed to feel and believe about myself; and "I can do this," the outcome I wanted. That is how my mantra became "I am safe. I am strong. I can do this."

In addition to using this technique myself, I've used this mantra formula with both my kids and my clients when they feel stuck while trying to change a behavior.

Sometime during the past sixteen years, my very capable daughter got the idea that she wasn't good at math. When she'd face a challenging math problem, she'd get frustrated and want to stop doing the work. For her, the mantra that worked went something like: "I am smart. I can learn. I will figure this out." This reset her nervous system in those moments and invited the problem-solving, learning-loving, challenge-facing part of her to the party.

I worked with a coaching client who routinely felt uncomfortable pitching her consulting services—which were an extension of her accomplishments—to potential clients. This discomfort stemmed from a root belief that if she tried to talk herself up, she'd come across as thinking she was better than other people. Intellectually, she knew that selling herself was part of selling her consulting services, but her nervous system didn't agree. When she knew that pitching her services was coming, her throat would tighten and her palms would sweat. She'd downplay her accomplishments and lean on the team and substantive product instead. She'd received repeated feedback that she conveyed a lack of confidence in herself and her consulting services. We worked together on a mantra. Her mantra was: "I can be great, that doesn't mean I'm better than others. I have worked hard for what I've achieved. I am allowed to talk about it." Again, this mantra served as a simple nervous system reset, allowing her to get unstuck and past this old belief.

The last step is to figure out when to deploy your mantra. It might be obvious—like it was with my daughter. When she slammed the book shut or was holding her head in her hands over her math homework, I knew it was time to remind her of her mantra. Or it might be more subtle, like it was with my coaching client—throat tightness, sweaty palms, or stomach knots can be clues that your nervous system is reverting to an old pattern. Once you have your mantra and you've identified the moment, you can recondition your nervous system to help you overcome your old belief. Armed with this simple formula, you can convert your nervous system from skeptic to ally.

Chapter 15

BREAKTHROUGH BEHAVIOR #8 ENLISTING SUPPORT

Finally, the last—and possibly most important thing—to remember as you strive to close your happiness gaps is that you are not alone. You are not designed to be alone. You are not designed to do life alone. Sometimes it will feel too heavy. And when it does, stop trying to carry it by yourself. Enlist support.

I am a lot of things: mother, wife, business owner, coach, part-time student, daughter, friend. But I am not a superwoman. I don't have mythical, magical, superhuman powers that allow me to carry everything with no fatigue, to magically heal from all illness and injury (emotional or physical), to fly, or to bend space and time. I am human. I hurt. I feel heavy sometimes. I get tired. Scars remain. I only have twenty-four hours in each day—just like every human—and I love to sleep.

Yet, all through my adult life, I've been told that I'm a superwoman. I know these comments were meant as compliments. And for a long time, I took them in that spirit—plus some. Being a superwoman became my identity. Becky can do anything. Becky can handle it. Becky is strong. Becky's got this. But friends, I am *not* a superhero. I'm not. Sometimes I can't do it, can't handle it, am not strong enough. Sometimes I need help. Sometimes I need a lot of help.

For a long time, I was afraid to ask for help, afraid to say I needed it, afraid to be vulnerable. Because, after all, I was supposed to be a superhero. Superheroes save the day; they don't need rescuing. But I am not a superhero. And neither are you. You are extraordinary, amazing, incomparable, and strong. You may even have some superpowers—like compassion, intelligence, love, kindness, empathy, or a wicked sense of humor. But you are not superhuman. You also need help sometimes: it's okay to ask for it. It's okay to be vulnerable. It's okay not to be okay.

During a particularly emotionally heavy period a couple of years ago, I was feeling exhausted and overwhelmed. Without realizing it, I was facing the end of one season and the beginning of another, which, in retrospect, I felt wholly unprepared for and was resisting with all my might. My husband was in the midst of his own transition and related challenges and I was feeling powerless to help him. At the same time, both kids were in the throes of transitioning to new schools. I knew I needed more support than I had—from family, from friends, and probably from mental health professionals. I was, however, hesitant to enlist that support. I am and always have been fiercely independent. In addition, I have always preferred to be in control. I was feeling decidedly out of control and asking for help from my support system felt like admitting I couldn't handle it alone. I didn't recognize these forces at the time; all I knew was that seeking out support—especially support that required my active participation (like verbally unpacking what I was dealing with)—felt impossible.

At the same time, I had been reading and learning more about the role of energy in our bodies, emotions, and lives. During my social media escapism, I ran across a local Facebook group post by a woman who had recently left her corporate IT job to pursue working as a Reiki healer full time. I had been curious about Reiki already, but her story really stood out. I, too, was in the throes of recognizing that my life calling would require stepping off the traditional path, a path I'd been raised to believe was the path for me. The post came and went. A week or two later, I dreamed I had made an appointment with this practitioner, and I woke up so excited. This was the final encouragement I needed to schedule an appointment. I went to my first Reiki session with exactly zero expectations. None. I was just excited I had an appointment with someone to "deal with my issues" but that, as I understood it, I would have to do nothing but lie there. I could handle this.

When I arrived for the appointment, Pratima asked me where in my body I was feeling tension or pain. And I told her all the usual places for someone who spends much of her day sitting in front of a computer: hips, lower back, shoulders, neck, jaw, and the constant nagging tension between my shoulder blades that sometimes made it difficult to take a deep breath. She suggested we start with my back and instructed me to lie facedown on her massage table. She then put on some relaxing music, rang some bells, and led me through a breathing exercise before we began. So far, this pretty much seemed like a trip to the spa. I was all for it.

A few minutes in, Pratima moved her hands over my back and settled them on that pesky point of pain between my shoulder blades. As she rested her hands there, I felt them get warmer and warmer and warmer. They were unnaturally warm. My practical self briefly considered whether this was too "woo woo" for me. But the part of me desperate for change decided to take a "what have you got to lose" approach and stick with this process a little longer. After a few minutes of lying there with her unnaturally warm hands on my back, I felt flooded with heat, felt an audible pop, and heard an inner voice say: *You don't have to carry it all.* Immediately the tension between my shoulder blades dissolved.

I get that this might sound weird or crazy. If I hadn't experienced it, I might not believe it either. Whether that voice was the Divine, my intuition, or wholly a figment of my imagination doesn't really matter. That voice was a powerful reminder—which came with a physical message—that I am not a superhero. It was a reminder that a heavy load is best borne by a team rather than an individual. I wasn't going to win any awards for carrying everything all the time by myself. It was time to lighten the load.

I didn't shift my behavior immediately. After several more sessions of Reiki, I was finally ready to engage in activities that required my active participation—such as working with a therapist and asking my friends for help. How I found support is not as important as what this story illustrates: support is beautiful, and be broad and creative in the ways you seek support. I will add that although I firmly believe in the necessity of support, I am still fiercely independent, prefer to be in control, and sometimes feel challenged to ask for help and support. These are works in progress. Yet I think of this experience often and remember that when life feels too heavy to carry alone, I don't have to. I can set it down or I can ask for help. So can you.

ACTION STEP:
LIGHTEN YOUR LOAD

Sharing the burden is one way to accomplish more but do less. For some of you—particularly those who have previously received praise for doing it all—this will be hard, and you may encounter some internal or external resistance. But if you want to do less and be more, you must get comfortable lightening your load. If you continue trying to do it all on your own, you will continue to live with the pain of carrying too much for too long. It might not show up at first, but it will catch up with you—the way carrying a heavy shopping bag is fine for a few steps but leaves painful marks on your hands if you have to walk too far. Your pain might live between your shoulder blades—as it did for me—or it might show up in other physical or emotional ways.

The need to evaluate your load is not a one-time exercise. It is a check-in you should do regularly. For example, I know when that nagging shoulder blade pain starts to resurface, it's a sign from my body to evaluate what I'm carrying and consider making a change.

You can deploy this action step now, or you can hold it in your arsenal for when you are trying to do too much alone. You can use the work you did in part I—your happiness recipe components—as the basis for this exercise and future check-ins.

To evaluate how you can lighten your load, consider the following questions:

What are you carrying right now that feels too heavy to carry?

In answering this question, recognize that you are in a safe space. Nobody is going to judge you if you feel like it is too much. Nobody is going to say you must do it all on your own or you have failed. You haven't failed: You are human, remember? Humans need other humans.

How can you lighten your load?

There are two ways to carry less: get help or set it down. Figure out how to lighten your load with these two related questions:

What can you set down?

Certain things we carry either can't be fixed or simply don't need to be carried right now. As you consider what is making your load heavier, consider whether you can set anything down. Setting it down doesn't mean you are quitting or can't come back to it later. It simply means you are making the conscious decision not to carry it right now. And guess what? You don't have to.

How can you enlist support from others?

The other way to lighten your load is to enlist the help of others. This includes everything from delegating and outsourcing to seeking support from service providers, such as mental health professionals. I recognize that practical and lifestyle limitations may shape how this can be executed. Being aware of how you would like to lighten your load— which sorts of people you'd like to enlist on your team—can help you identify and prioritize your resources. In this step, you should cast a wide and creative net—get curious about who you might enlist beyond the network you've traditionally called upon. For me that was Reiki—what could it be for you? Finally, don't forget that this list can also include your relationship with the Divine. For people who have a belief in a power greater than them—for me, it's God—this can be an invitation to reconnect or rekindle that relationship.

What is one thing you can remove from your load to be immediately happier?

Consider for a moment what you are spending emotional or physical energy on, which, if you could eliminate it, would immediately support greater happiness. Maybe you've identified this thing above, but maybe you haven't. It doesn't need to be big or emotional. For me, it was the five a.m. wake-up with the dogs. I wouldn't have mentioned it in any exercise above, but when my husband, who is unapologetically a morning person, took on primary responsibility for getting up with the dogs at five a.m., my happiness increased significantly—especially in proportion to the amount of effort required from him. Big wins with small downsides are the best. I'd encourage you to think about those things in your life that you perceive as necessary or routine, but that are a drain on your happiness. Consider whether you can cancel them, share them, or at least reduce them. And then when you figure that out, do it as soon as possible.

In this life, we are meant to be connected to others. We are meant to be supported, guided, and loved. We need to unlearn the lesson that doing it alone means we are better or more successful. We need to learn that shared success is just as valuable as individual success. Finally, we need to learn that it is not a problem to admit when we need help. That it is okay to admit that we are struggling. That it is okay to enlist support. In fact, we need to learn that it is an absolute necessity to lighten our load so that we can truly live a priority-aligned life.

PART III

THE PHYSICAL ENERGY GAP

Before I got good at editing my expenditures of time, resources, and money, my to-do list would have been titled: "From Here to Eternity." I'd never get through my whole list. Making the list itself sometimes took center stage—even over the doing. It's always been easy for me to see what needs to get done to reach a goal or arrive at a destination. I can very quickly break a project down into actionable steps. And I love lists. What I've needed to work on, however, is subtracting. I'm not talking about the kind of subtraction you learned in elementary school. I am talking about the kind of subtraction where you remove things from your list that aren't critical to your happiness. Remember, the happiness recipe is simple—do more of what matters, do less of the rest. I've always been pretty good at doing more—so once I knew what to do more of, I could do it. I wasn't so skilled at "less of the rest." I wasn't familiar with having space in my schedule. I wasn't familiar with life beyond overwhelm. My biggest challenge was subtraction.

Something shifted when I realized that spending time on anything besides what matters most to me is me effectively saying no to what matters. If I say yes to those other things, I am using capacity (time, energy, and resources) that is now unavailable for what matters. And I realized that is backward: I want to say yes to what matters and no to the rest. The primary tool I use to accomplish this is subtracting. Now when I make a to-do list, there are two steps to the process—make the list, then subtract the things that don't support the most important things in my life. And when I schedule my time, same thing—remove what takes time away from the most important things in my life.

If this sounds terrifying, don't worry. Remind yourself it's simply your nervous system speaking up to remind you that you are doing something different. Moreover, the following chapters will give you the structure you need to make this happen. You will start by getting clear on your priorities. You have a map of what matters, but what you don't have is order. And order is how you begin to build a system that will make life, decision-making, and action taking much easier. The first step to creating order is to identify your top priority for this season—one season, one top priority. Then you can consider the other things that matter and put them in order. This order will help you choose between competing priorities and evaluate where and when to spend your time, energy, and resources.

Once you have this list, you can begin to take focused action, in the form of concrete to-dos or habit building. Which approach you deploy will depend on whether you are trying to *do, have,* or *be* something. Next, we'll teach your nervous system to let go of perfection and provide continuous motivation—so that you can create lasting change. Finally, you'll discover how to measure your success and know when you've made meaningful progress on what matters most to you.

This is where the rubber meets the road—and I know some of you are excited. You are ready. If that is you, please remember to slow down and really consider how you'll use the space you've created in your schedule to support your highest priorities. Some of you are not excited. You are wondering how you will get everything done and make lasting change. If that is you, just remember, all you need to do is take one step at a time. You don't have to finish the trip in one day—all you need to do is drive.

Chapter 16

IN ORDER

Before you jump into closing your Physical Energy Gap through action, there's one last thing you need to do. Of all the things you want to have or do in this season, you need to identify the one that is most important to you. That's right, I said "the one." This will be the thing that takes precedence above all things. And yes, for this season, there can only be one thing. However, that doesn't mean you are throwing out or abandoning the rest. After you identify your top priority, you need to figure out where the other pieces will fall. You are working on living a priority-aligned life, after all, so charging forward without clarity on the rank and order of what you want in your current season would just be perpetuating your Physical Energy Gap— where you spend time on things that aren't important to you and don't increase your happiness as a result.

I want to say it again because it is really important—you can only have one top priority. If you are feeling like this is too rigid and you want a more flexible list, I have two responses: (1)

you are in charge of your list, *but* (2) if you can adopt this one rule as rigidly as possible—one component in each slot—then you will have a framework for decision-making and problem-solving that really does make life easier. You will never have to stop and figure out what is most important right now, you will already know.

Let me give you a few examples. As I've said, during my Working Motherhood Season, my family was my top priority. Because I was clear on this, because I was committed to this, and because I applied this rule pretty rigidly, it was easy to make decisions. When circumstances asked me to choose between work and family, nine times out of ten, I chose family—without hesitation and without guilt. And the one time I didn't, guilt or unhappiness would start to seep in.

Now let's consider a more global example. When COVID-19 hit, things shut down in many parts of the world. People who weren't essential workers were told to stay home—to make their health and community their new top priority. By contrast, essential workers were told that their work was the top priority. This is where it gets interesting. Some people accepted these new priorities. Other people didn't—they felt the tension between their personal priorities and this more global priority. And what was the outcome of that tension? You guessed it . . . unhappiness. I am making no statement about the right or wrong response—rather, I'm asking you to observe what happens when tension between priorities is created.

I want to tell you about Alexis. Alexis was a graduate student, had a full-time job (in which she was anticipating a promotion), and was in a new marriage. Alexis was overwhelmed. We did a version of the taking-stock, mapping, and connecting exercises in the prior chapters. Through this work, she identified that she wanted to ensure she had couple time, time to engage in training and development opportunities at work, and time to network as much as possible in her master's program. She felt better just having this list. A couple of weeks after developing this list, we met for another session. She was frustrated. She knew her areas of focus, but she was struggling when her priorities conflicted with each other. She couldn't quickly and easily figure out, for example, how to choose between the evening networking event and dinner with her husband, or between the lunch-and-learn at her graduate school and the training class at work. Of course she was struggling—she hadn't finished the work. She hadn't put these three areas of focus in priority order.

I asked her which of these three areas was most important. This was difficult for Alexis to answer. She loved her husband and wanted her marriage to succeed. But she also wanted greater professional opportunities, either through work or through her master's program. Success in these areas would also benefit her marriage. As she struggled through these issues, I reminded Alexis of two things. First, that she only needed to prioritize in *this* season—and that, as seasons changed, her priorities might also. Second, that there was no wrong answer—only her answer. If she wanted to put networking first, she could. And if she wanted to put her marriage first, she could. It was truly up to her. After exploring some of her stories and other people's shoulds, she concluded that, for her, being present in her marriage was the top priority. She committed to working with her husband to identify ways they could focus on strengthening their relationship.

When she returned for her next session, Alexis told me that she and her husband agreed that Saturday was their day. They wouldn't make plans to do anything else or take on any other commitments on Saturday. Second, they agreed that two nights a week they would cook dinner at home and watch a couple of hours of TV together. Rather than setting specific days, they agreed to talk—on Saturday—about the schedule for the coming week. She reported that her husband loved that she was putting their marriage first, and that articulating it as a priority—backed up with a concrete plan—had reduced her decision-making stress tenfold. Alexis found freedom in prioritizing. So can you.

In the exercise below, you will be asked to make some hard decisions. You may never have declared only one thing to be your top priority. People usually resist until they see the power that "keeping the main thing the main thing" can provide. People don't like doing this because they worry that they might hurt someone or that someone in their life will judge their choice—as my mom may have worried when she told us that work was her top priority or as I did when I told my parents that parenthood was mine. Remind yourself that you aren't looking for other people's answers to your happiness— you are trying to find your own happiness recipe. In this exercise, this means the only shoulds that matter are the ones that matter to you. Taking this leap, considering only what matters to you and letting go of the rest, is much easier said than done. But I've witnessed its success dozens of times—in my own life, in my friends' lives, and with my clients—so I know that while it may be difficult, it is possible.

ACTION STEP:
PRIORITIES

Step One: There can only be one top priority. Identify it.

Those puzzle pieces you've been gathering form the foundations of this exercise—the list from which your top priority will come. Identifying the one thing that will matter most to you in this season may come easily. It may have been obvious to you when I said the words "top priority" at the beginning of this chapter. Equally, your answer may not immediately feel clear. You may need to do some exploring of your list to determine what matters most to you in this season. And that exploration may take time.

Usually, people can at least narrow it down to the top two to four items. If you are stuck there, consider making the choice slightly more concrete. Ask yourself, *If I had a time conflict and had to pick between these options, how would I decide and what would I choose?* For example, let's say you have three items on your list: "fitness," "job advancement," and "time with parents." You could imagine a situation in which you were asked to work more hours on a project that would guarantee a promotion but would also mean giving up your daily workout plans and missing your weekly dinner with your parents for several weeks or months. Consider what you would do. Would you work the extra hours because the promotion is your top priority? Or would you set a boundary with work, letting them know that while you are happy to work on the project, you aren't available before eight a.m. (so you can keep your workout) or on Wednesday evenings (so you can keep your dinner plans).

You might be reading this hypothetical situation thinking: *This isn't really a choice; I can't say no to work.* But here's the deal, you *can* say no to work. There will just be consequences. The question really is: Can you live with the consequences? If not, your top priority may be work—either the promotion or just staying gainfully employed. Either way, own that priority. Failing to own your priority, whatever it is, will just reopen that Authenticity Gap you've worked so hard to close.

Step Two: Rank the rest.

Good news! You don't have to throw out the rest of the list and only focus on your top priority for the rest of this season. You do, however, need to figure out the relative priority of the rest of the items. As you do this, acknowledge that lower priority items may see less progress during this season and that's to be expected. Sometimes lower priority items feel solid already or are those around which you already have solid habits that you can continue—things that don't need a lot of extra care and feeding. You'll have only one top priority, only one second priority, only one third priority, and so on. Don't put everything else second. I am asking you to rank the rest because having an order and a structure does two things. It helps you make decisions when conflicts arise. You know what matters most, so you can do what matters most. And by matching your physical energy to your top priority, you can close the Physical Energy Gap for good.

The result of this exercise should be a list in ranked order (most important to least important) of the things you need to be happy during this season of your life. If it's the first time you have done an activity like this, give yourself some grace. You may find as you begin to take action that, in fact, number four is really number six, and number six is really number four. That's okay. This list isn't a contract, it's a guide. More than that: this list is yours. If it needs to change or adjust—then adjust it. Be wary, however, any time you make a significant change to numbers one through three. Those are big changes, and changing your top three priorities may signal you are entering a new season. In addition, while this is your list and you can do anything you want, if your top three priorities are moving targets, you will struggle against continued unhappiness from your unresolved Physical Energy Gap.

As you move forward with the work in this book—and take priority-aligned action—you will be focused on your top priority more than most other things in your life. That is to be expected, because it's your top priority. It doesn't mean you will stop doing everything else—you will likely have time and space to focus on other ranked priorities. But it does mean that you will be removing the noise that has distracted you from happiness up until this point. You will be saying no; you will be removing what doesn't matter. This change doesn't need to happen overnight—this change can and will take time. Besides thinking about what you want to do, you also need to decide what you don't want to do and, therefore, say no to.

Unless you picked up this book already knowing exactly what you wanted, how to get there, and in what order, you have done a lot of work to get to this point. Before we jump into the action taking, pause for a moment and appreciate what you've done. You have probably confronted some new and uncomfortable emotions. You were honest with yourself in ways you haven't been before. You have dreamed bigger and bolder than you have in the past. And I know you are that much closer to being happier in your life right now. Breathe in this growth and change. Be thankful for how far you've come. And get excited about what's next.

Chapter 17

ACTION PLAN

You've identified what you want and what you need to do to get there. You understand the barriers, in the form of your old beliefs and feelings, that may have kept you from reaching your desired destination up until now. Based on the work you did over the last several chapters, you now have your happiness recipe. You have in front of you a list, in order, of what you want to have or achieve to be as happy as possible in your current season. This list contains things that matter to you—not anyone else's shoulds. This list contains what you want now, not later. And this list is possible. Now it's time to give shape to the actions you must take to make this picture of happiness a reality.

I want to be clear: while we'll focus on your top priority (more on that in the next chapter), you might also explore action steps for other things on your list. You might be expecting me to say something like: "Now it's time to set some goals," but I'm not going to say it. Don't get me wrong, goals have a place—they just don't belong everyplace. For me, goals have been more of a form-over-substance activity. Another box to check to prove that I've accomplished something. Because this was my approach, achieving goals didn't necessarily help me achieve my desires. For example, let's say I set a goal of one weekly date night and resolutely stuck to making it happen because it was specific, measurable, achievable, and I could check it off. But if this only focused me on the task and not the deeper why—what outcome this date served (i.e., more connection in my marriage)—then the goal didn't serve me. Too often, achieving our goals becomes about checking the boxes instead of actually getting where we want to go. I have found that I do better thinking about my actions in terms of what I want to achieve, then focusing on small daily ways to move in that direction.

Here's another way to think about your forward progress: instead of setting a goal, map yourself to a destination. Imagine your movement forward is like a road trip. You are trying to get from Virginia (where you are today) to California (where you want to be in this season of your life or in preparation for the next season). You recognize actions must be taken to move from point A to point B. And yes, you could set goals like: "Exit Virginia by next week and drive across West Virginia by next month." But those goals wouldn't necessarily tell you what you need to do today. And if you are like me, if you failed to hit one or two of the milestone goals, you'd be at risk of scrapping the whole trip. By focusing on a destination, I find it is easier for me to keep the ultimate desire in mind and to redirect, reset, and rest when I need to. If goal setting has worked for you in the past, then by all means carry on. Use the tools that work for you. But if goal setting hasn't gotten you where you want to go—consider this destination-mapping approach instead.

When Sam and I began working together, he wanted to transform his career entirely. He wanted to leave his nonprofit job and start a graphic design business. But he wasn't sure where to start. Over several coaching sessions, he grew frustrated because he felt that until he left his current job, he couldn't make any progress toward achieving the dream he knew would make him happy. But leaving his job was not a financially viable option for him in the short term. In other words, Sam had decided that until he achieved his goal (quitting his public interest job), any progress he made in the direction of graphic design didn't count.

I suggested that Sam consider his move toward a new career as a journey, not a goal, and that he could and was, in fact, making progress, even if he hadn't quit his public interest job yet. For example, when Sam did graphic design projects on the weekends for friends and family, he was building a portfolio of work. Or when he attended an online class in the evening, he was increasing his skills. And even when he saved money by not eating out as much, he was taking an incremental step in the direction of his dream. This caused an immediate shift. Sam could then quickly identify the action steps he could take to move him toward his destination. Instead of being hung up on how quickly he was or wasn't getting there, he could simply focus on driving each day, knowing that if he kept going, he'd get there.

Like Sam, many of us have big dreams, and when those dreams seem out of reach, we get frustrated or even give up. If you are looking at your happiness recipe now and feeling daunted by what's on that list, take heart. Remember where you are going and recognize that to get there, you only need to drive in that direction each day. Next, we'll map out the beginning of your trip.

ACTION STEP:
ROUTE MAP

For each ingredient of your happiness recipe—the map you generated at the end of part I—starting with the top priority and working your way down the list, walk through the steps below:

Step One: Consider which components of your list require tasks and which might require new habits.

Before we jump into your action plan, let's add one other layer for your consideration. As you review the ingredients in your happiness recipe, think about whether they are things you want to *do* and *have*, or *be*. For example, in this season, I want to *have* a full roster of clients, but I want to *be* physically fit. This difference is important. For what you want to *have*, you'll want to define the next aligned actions. By contrast, for what you want to *be*, you'll need to build new habits—something we will address later. Some components of your list might require both tasks and habits. For example, I want to have less unsmart debt. That will require me to change my spending habits and take aligned action.

Review each ingredient and determine whether it requires actions, habits, or both. This will help you figure out how to approach each area going forward. Put those ingredients that clearly require new habits aside for now. We will address them soon. For things you want to *have* or *do*, continue working through the action steps below.

Step Two: Identify the next three to five things you must do to support each task-driven component on your list.

If it helps, think of this as the beginning of your trip—the things you'll need to do to get going and where you will go first. This doesn't have to be complicated or revolutionary. Simply come up with a list of things you need to do to start moving you toward your destination. For example, as I started my current season, one of the things I wanted to *have* was a thriving coaching business that serves lots of people through group and one-on-one coaching. When I started this journey, I was thinking only about how to launch. At the early outset, my next steps included getting my coaching certification, having a brand, and leveraging my network. Obviously, these three things were more-project-level statements. You may want to dig deeper into more specific next steps. For example, on a more micro level, leveraging my network looked like: (1) developing a concise statement of the kind of client I was looking for, (2) making a list of people to contact, and (3) doing at least five reach-outs daily. Drill down here as much as needed to make the step actionable. Ultimately, it's helpful to turn projects into bite-size steps, but for the purposes of this chapter, identifying more generally where action is needed is a great start.

Step Three: Consider whether there's anything you need to do those things but don't have.

In keeping with the road trip analogy, these are the things you need to travel—like gas, car, good tunes, or comfortable clothes. What might you need to get started that you don't already have? No need to list out everything you'll ever need, just what's needed for the first few action steps. Continuing with the example above, to launch my business, I needed a website (which I didn't have) and I needed clients (to complete my certification hours). I didn't need to hire an assistant or a bunch of employees—maybe someday I would, but not during the early part of my journey.

The action steps you identify here will become the basis for developing your daily task list. By focusing on what you need to do first and now, rather than what you might need to do someday, you can take priority-aligned action on a daily, weekly, and monthly basis. As you begin to accomplish these milestones, you can revisit this exercise to continue to map toward your dreams.

Chapter 18

ONE STEP AT A TIME

I suspect you are looking at the top three to five items in your happiness recipe and thinking about all the things you need to do to get closer to having them. As you consider jumping in and taking action, you might find yourself thinking:

I can't do this. This is overwhelming; there is so much to do and so much that can get in the way. Maybe this was a bad idea.

I don't know where to start. I was feeling great, but now I don't know; I'm just not sure what to do next.

I'm so excited; let's get going. I'm going to do all the things, right now!

No matter which best describes you, what you need to do next is the same. Just start driving. Just go. And after you finish today's driving, you will wake up tomorrow and drive some more—it might be a little bit, it might be a lot. If you keep moving in the general direction of your destination, you will get there. If you don't, you probably won't. Sound too simple? Wondering why you paid for this book when the answer is "Just go do it"? Because it is simple, but that doesn't mean it's easy. And it's always better to start with simple.

Take your top priority—the *one* thing most important to your happiness in this season—and look at the action steps required to achieve it. When you look at those action steps, you may see a natural order to them. Or you may find yourself drawn toward whatever feels easiest to accomplish first. Before you jump in, consider whether something in your list of action items might be the one thing that makes everything easier. Highlight it. If you are moving toward a destination that is quite different from where you are today, please know that doing the one thing that makes everything easier might also feel really big.

When I decided to finally leave my job and start my own business, I didn't tell anyone. Well, that isn't exactly true—I had a couple of consulting clients who knew I had my own business because I was working with them. What I told no one, other than a few friends and family, was that I was going to get certified as an executive coach. I had been a leader of people my whole career, and practically speaking, I had been coaching, guiding, and mentoring for decades—without any formal training or certifications. But I hadn't officially claimed it. After attending the on-campus portion of the Executive Coaching Certificate Program at the University of California, Berkeley, I considered how I was going to launch my coaching business. I made a list of potential action steps—building my website, reaching out to a few select friends, updating my LinkedIn bio, and posting on social media.

To me, building my website seemed the most tangible, and I believed it would help me seem more legitimate. (Raise your hand if you think I was feeling slightly insecure.) I built my website and then it was time to update my LinkedIn bio and announce it to everyone. In that moment I realized two things: I was terrified, and I was about to do the thing that would change everything. By telling everyone in my personal and professional networks that I was a coach, I was officially claiming my destination for the next season. I did not anticipate how scary that would be—I was 100 percent clear on where I wanted to go, I had no doubt, but now I was going to announce it to the world. And that was going to change everything.

As you evaluate your first step, I hope you feel braver than I did—I hope you do the thing that changes everything (if you can identify it) first. If you can't see it yet or aren't ready yet, then just drive. And when you finish that first thing, then do the next thing. Continue to focus your time and energy on moving toward what matters most to you, one thing at a time, one day at a time. As you drive, keep an eye out for opportunities to supercharge your progress—in my experience, they usually come in the form of action steps that feel scary and big. Remember, those scary feelings may just be your nervous system's way of confirming that you are, in fact, growing.

ACTION STEP:
PICK A STARTING POINT

In chapter 16 you identified your top priority for this season. In chapter 17 you identified what your behavior would need to look like if you had this thing—in other words, what you would need to *do* to reach this destination. Now it's time to start. This action step is deceptively simple.

Step One: Identify your first action step.

All you need to do is select one thing you can do right now—in whole or in part—to move you in the direction of your desired destination. One thing. Simply answer the question: What can I do today to move me closer to happiness?

Step Two: Do the thing.

It's all well and good to identify the thing, to put it on your list, to recognize that you need to do it. Doing it is often a wholly different matter. If you are feeling resistance to actually doing the action, consider the source of that resistance. Does the action require you to think or believe something you aren't entirely comfortable with yet? Or are you simply feeling growing pains? Either way, check out the chapters in part II for some ideas on how to overcome this resistance.

This is where I have seen so many people get tripped up. They get excited about what they want to accomplish but get overwhelmed by what it will take to get there. The overwhelm happens for one of two reasons—either they see the whole trip laid out before them or they just don't even know where to start. Overcoming both barriers happens the same way: by starting. By picking one thing, doing it, and seeing what happens.

Returning to our Virginia-to-California road trip analogy, whether you start by loading the car, driving the car, or walking in the direction of California, you are making progress. If you start and find you've gotten off course or aren't pointed in the right direction, you can redirect and keep going. If you discover you need something you don't have, you can take a detour to get it. Because I am so convinced that just starting is the key to finishing, I end most of my coaching sessions with three questions:

1. What are you going to do next?
2. When are you going to do it?
3. How do you want me to hold you accountable?

You can also use these questions and seek accountability from someone in your life—a friend, a mentor or even a coach. Ultimately, progress happens when you take action every day. Even the longest journey can be broken into a series of single inches. If you know where you are going, all you need to do is continue to move in that direction—consistently.

Chapter 19

DAILY DECISIONS, LONG-TERM RESULTS

In working with clients to change their lives, I often see people make a simple mistake—they confuse tasks with habits. They decide they want to *do* something—for example, lose weight, meditate more, or stop being late to meetings—when really what they need is to *be* something. And as a result, they think adding tasks to their to-do list or appointments to their calendar will get them to their desired destination. No doubt allocating time for a new behavior is part of the solution, but these types of changes aren't a project with an end date, these changes are *habits*.

As we've discussed, I love a good to-do list. Nothing brings me joy like checking off the things I've done. I used to chronically add to my to-do list all the tasks I felt I should be doing, only to fail to check them off at the end of the day or week. Each time I failed to check off those things I should have been doing, I felt like a failure. Sometimes in small ways and sometimes in big ways. These things included: work out, meditate, drink more water, and eat lunch (something I especially struggled with after I started working from home). As I considered these to-do list failures, I recognized that these were habits I needed to cultivate, not one-time actions I could check off a list. In other words, I was choosing a task when I needed a habit.

In addition, I wasn't acting like these habits mattered a whole lot to me. I said they did, but I was not living that statement. Resolving this issue required getting super honest with myself. I took those recurrent to-do list failures and had a serious internal dialogue about whether those things were important to me or not. If they were important, I needed to close the Physical Energy Gap and choose to make daily time for them. If they were not important in this season, I needed to release any feelings of failure associated with not doing them. For me, this internal dialogue has become a crucial part of living a priority-aligned life.

For example, in 2018 I went through a period where I started and then quit workout program after workout program. I'd start strong—jumping in with two feet to complete daily workouts that were well above my fitness level. Then I'd get sore, busy, or tired and I'd miss a workout and then another. Focusing on the workouts I'd missed, I'd stop working out altogether only to pick up and restart the process a couple of weeks later. I think I did the first two weeks of one particular program four or five times that year. This wasn't an effective cycle.

I decided to get honest with myself. Although I genuinely wanted to be healthier and more fit, at this particular time in my life, it was not my top priority. It wasn't even in my top five. I knew that given my history with weight, fitness, and wellness, to change this behavior and become a regular exerciser would require a level of commitment I wasn't prepared to give. I was not destined, in this season, to be the fittest I could possibly be. And that was okay, because it wasn't important to me at that moment. I could continue to make healthy choices about what I put in my body and I could move when it felt right. But I didn't need to beat myself up about not achieving my daily dose of activity. And I certainly didn't need to, and frankly couldn't, commit to a multiweek high-intensity daily workout program. I knew I wanted to change this someday, but I also knew this wasn't the right moment and maybe it wasn't even the right season.

By contrast, at the end of 2019, I wanted to develop a meditation habit, as soon as possible. A meditation dabbler for years, I recently discovered that when I meditated, I was actually a better person. At that time, I was facing a bunch of choices as I launched my business, and I believed that regular meditation would help me quiet my mind and make better decisions. I also knew that my track record for creating new habits was not the strongest. I sought some help. Help came in the form of *Atomic Habits* by James Clear. That book offers great guidance about setting habits. There were, however, two pieces of advice that changed everything for me. The first: if you are starting a habit of meditating, for example, you need to redefine your identity to include the idea that you are "someone who meditates." This shift is key because if you are someone who meditates and you miss a day or two or even three, you pick meditation right back up again. You don't quit meditating because you failed to meditate every day or because you had a few bad days. After all, you're a meditator and meditators meditate. The second piece of advice is to start small. Because I love to-do lists and checking things off, I've always approached things like meditation as a task with a deadline, and therefore, I'd start huge and then burn out. Now that I understood that a habit is something you become, I also understood that it is best to start small and grow—like a snowball.

My meditation habit went like this. I declared that I, Becky, am a meditator. Then I made a commitment that I would meditate sometime in the day before bed—or no sleep for me. I didn't require myself to meditate in the morning (though I knew that was ultimately what I wanted to build toward) or for a particular length of time. I just committed to meditating. Some days that looked like waking up and meditating for fifteen to twenty minutes. Other days, it looked like focused breathing on the bathroom bench for two minutes after brushing my teeth at ten thirty p.m. Still other days, it was somewhere in between.

But you know what? The days I meditated quickly outnumbered the days I didn't. In addition, I noticed I felt much clearer and much more able to perform during my day if I started it with meditation. So if I didn't do my morning meditation and started to feel sluggish, anxious, or overwhelmed by decisions, I'd stop and meditate. And miraculously nearly 100 percent of the time my day would improve. Soon the last-ditch bathroom-bench focused breathing happened much less frequently, and I was consistently meditating earlier and earlier in the day. Approaching a habit this way—as something you build and then become—actually made adopting a new habit a relatively painless experience. My nervous system appreciated the regular wins and my mind appreciated the meditation.

You can use these two powerful pieces of advice to build your habits, too. If this advice alone doesn't cut it or you just want to learn more about habit creation, I highly recommend *Atomic Habits*.

ACTION STEP:
BUILD A HABIT

If you have decided that to live a more priority-aligned life, you need to build some new habits, try these five steps.

Step One: Identify your new identity.

Remember, habits aren't tasks, they are something you are. To figure out what that means for you, ask yourself:

That thing I want to do, what does it mean about who I am?

Once you figure out what your new identity includes, claim it. If you are feeling really brave, tell a friend or family member.

Step Two: Realize there is no timeframe for completion.

Habits don't have a deadline. When you are building a new habit, you are trying, I presume, to create a behavior change that will become permanent. You won't be able to complete the habit—so there's no rush. If that feels hard, overwhelming, or scary, remind yourself you can't fail unless you die. Literally. If you keep chipping away at this habit, you will eventually get there.

Step Three: Start small.

You've identified the habit, now figure out what you are going to do to start. Make it a *micro*step: big enough to notice, but so small it almost seems silly in its smallness—like putting your exercise clothes on but not requiring any exercise, or reading one page of a book, or carrying an empty water bottle around. To build your small step, ask yourself:

What is one small thing I can do to start acting more like a person who (fill in your new identity here)?

Then do it and only it for a short period of time—three days to two weeks is usually a good start, but trust your gut. For big changes, you might need to ease into things; for smaller changes, you might be able to go a little faster. Evaluate whether your wish to go faster is coming from a desire to be done or become. If you just want to be done, keep going, small and gradual, and remember you can't be done with a habit, you can only become.

Step Four: Build.

Once you've managed to complete the small first step, add to it. Remember, this is a forever thing, so stay with micro-steps if you need to. The simple goal is to do more than you were doing before. If you were reading one page of a book every day, maybe you increase that to ten minutes or ten pages (depending on your destination). If you were carrying an empty water bottle around, you fill it and track how much you drink—no requirement, no goal, just measurement.

Step Five: Measure to grow.

Someone once told me, "What gets measured gets corrected." Another way to approach behavior change is simply to measure the behavior. If you are feeling stuck in your habit building, this technique might help you get unstuck. I bet if you start tracking, you'll start improving—that has always been the case for me. Once you are in a good cadence of behaviors big enough to be measured, measure them. Keep track of how much water you drink, or how many pages you read, or how many minutes of activity you do. Just keep track. That's it. Don't judge, don't set a goal, just measure and see what happens.

In sum, depending on your priorities, you might need to build a new habit to get where you want to go. Recognizing when you need a habit instead of just action is important to empowering behavior change. Habits don't expire and you can't rush through them. When building a new habit, it's fine to build it slowly. In fact, starting small ensures you will have the stamina to become the person you want to become.

Chapter 20

FANCY CELEBRATIONS

As you move toward your destination, two things can help make your journey more pleasant—letting go of perfection and having some fun. Because growth and change are not linear, there will be times you aren't perfect. Some days you'll backtrack, or it won't feel easy to live the priority-aligned life you've designed. That doesn't mean you are doing it wrong—that just means you are human. Allow yourself to be human; focus on progress rather than perfection. And then, to keep it fun, find ways to celebrate your progress as often as possible.

In case it isn't already clear, we are a basketball family. I've spent more hours in a basketball gym than I care to count (and I've enjoyed most of them). I've watched two kids go from being so small that the basketball was bigger than their head to being teenagers with a mastery of the game. One unassailable reality of basketball is that any non-free-throw basket made from inside the three-point arc is worth two points. It doesn't matter whether you do a fancy dribble move, a sick spin, an ankle-breaking crossover, a highlight-worthy slam dunk, or you simply lay the ball in the basket—each basket is worth two points. I have seen child after child, including my own, try to be fancy, try to add some additional flair to their scoring opportunity. And I've seen them miss out on scoring two points as a result. I've seen them take their focus away from the real priority—putting the ball in the basket—and put it on looking good.

In much of life, as in basketball, it is almost always better to be finished than fancy. After all, at the end of the day, it's not the team with the prettiest baskets that wins, it's the team with the most points. And in a close game, the crowd cheers just as loud for the simple layup as they do for the dunk. In life, like on the basketball court, often people let perfect (or fancy) be the enemy of done. They get so focused on doing it perfectly that they fail to recognize that doing it—fancy or not—is almost always enough. This means two things for you as you move along this path: it's time to let go of perfectionism, and every time you score, you need to celebrate.

If you have spent your life being rewarded for performance—the best grades, the perfectly edited briefs, the errorless memos—it can be hard for you (and your nervous system) to recognize this is both a gift and a curse. It is a gift when there is value in perfection—for example delivering an errorless memo to a client may actually keep that client a client. But attempting to write an errorless first draft of this book, for example, when I am certain there will be future edits, will just slow me down. In fact, focusing on perfection rather than creativity may affirmatively hurt the final product. Even if there are missed errors in the final draft, it's probably going to be just fine. (In fact, if you find one, reach out to me and tell me about it. Then, together, we can celebrate the fact that I finished this book imperfectly and survived.)

Letting go of perfection is particularly important when you are learning a new skill. Consider a toddler: they don't need to know how to walk gracefully before they get up and try. They just get up, fall down, and get back up again—until at some point they have more or less mastered walking. The same skill building process applies to adults.

Let me tell you about Daniel. Daniel was in a new leadership position that required he handle more high-profile meetings than ever before. Daniel had demonstrated that he was prepared and capable. But these meetings were stressful. Daniel learned to pay attention to his Indicator Light, and he realized these meetings were a big trigger for him. And because his nervous system was not feeling safe, it called on one of its favorite defenses—perfectionism. Daniel spent extra time and energy preparing for these meetings so he could be sure they would go perfectly. Guess what, they rarely went perfectly. In one of our coaching sessions, as Daniel talked about overpreparing for another one of these meetings, I asked, "What would it look like if this meeting didn't go perfectly?" He answered, "Pretty much like all the other meetings that we've had before. They never go perfectly." My response: "So, you can't really mess it up, huh?" He laughed and realized that, yes, he was ready for these meetings and that even if things didn't go perfectly, everything would be fine. "You can't mess it up" became the mantra that he fed his nervous system to help calm it and to get out of the cycle of overpreparation and perfectionism.

As you start traveling toward your destination, please give yourself permission to finish without risking getting tripped up in being fancy. You might not be the first one to cross a state line or the best driver, but getting where you're going is ultimately what matters. Recognize that your desire to be perfect is probably your nervous system indicating that it's uncomfortable with what you are doing. The good news: now you know this is actually a *positive* thing—this discomfort is evidence that you are moving and growing.

ACTION STEP:
REFLECTIONS ON PERFECTION

To get in touch with your inner fancy maker, journal for a few minutes on each of these prompts (remember, *journal* is just code for *engage with*—do it in a way that feels comfortable for you).

When do I feel like I need to be perfect?

Where do I think the need to be perfect comes from?

How can I honor the idea that done is better than fancy (or perfect)?

Perfection can be a big hurdle—but it's also one you can overcome. Your perfectionism is completely within your control. Your perfectionism, though you may not feel like it, is a choice. You can choose finished over fancy. And, if you aren't used to it, your old nervous system rule might pop up—but that's okay. You can choose to make a new rule.

Now, let's talk about celebration. I am terrible at this. Truly. I'm much better at dwelling on what has gone or might go wrong. But I'm actively working on it. And as I've worked on incorporating more celebration into my life, I've noticed that when I celebrate the little wins, more wins follow. I've also noticed when I dwell on the downside, things tend to go south more quickly. This isn't really surprising in light of all the mounting evidence that emotions have a vibration and that our emotional frequency might actually attract things that match that frequency.

I can remember being so excited for little things as a child—seeing a friend, killing it on a quiz, a positive comment from a teacher, finding a pretty flower. Somewhere along the way, I grew out of enjoying the little moments. I've made a conscious effort to get back to more celebration. Celebrating the little things might seem silly at first, but give it a chance. Perhaps even consider leaning into the silly. For example, when I finish this section, I will have hit my word count for the day. To be clear, I'm nowhere near finished with this book. But I did the driving I needed to do today to move in the direction of my desired destination. You can bet I'm going to do something to celebrate. Today it will probably be as simple as putting on some upbeat music and dancing around my office. I might look goofy doing it—but frankly that makes it more fun.

Let's talk a little bit about why celebrations and rewards matter. They matter because they matter to your nervous system. The concept is pretty simple: when we do something that feels good, our brain releases chemicals, which magnify the good feelings. The actual mechanism and roles of the different happy-making chemicals are more complicated. Just know that when you celebrate *or* reward yourself, you are likely causing your brain to release one of those powerful chemicals. And know that your brain likes when these happy-makers are released and will typically seek more. This can be bad—it's the basis for some addictions and it's the reason you waste hours playing the latest app. It can also be good, providing the reason to stay motivated and keep going.

Now let's talk about the difference between rewards celebrations and microcelebrations. Back to our basketball analogy—microcelebrations are the cheers that happen with

every basket or good play; reward celebrations are the parties after a big win. Generally, people are pretty good—not
great—at reward celebrations. And generally, when it comes to
microcelebrations, people are inconsistent at best and terrible
at worst. This is problematic because if we only celebrate at
the point of reward, we aren't giving our brain the continuous
nudge to release the happy-making chemicals that motivate us
to keep making changes and actually reach the reward.

Think of a reward as something that you give yourself at
a big milestone—you lost X pounds, you paid off Y debt, you
finished the big project, you got a new job. Rewards may be
something you buy, an experience you give yourself, or somewhere that you go. They can also be delayed—you put in a lot
of work to earn them, and then, even when you reach the milestone, it might be a few days or even weeks before the payout.
Finally, rewards may have a financial cost, but it doesn't have
to be a big dollar amount. A reward can be something like
treating yourself to a pedicure or a nice dinner. But it can also
be a high-ticket item. A honeymoon is a perfect example—it's
the reward for finding someone you want to spend the rest of
your life with, planning a wedding, and taking the leap of getting married. There is nothing wrong with rewards. They just
don't happen frequently enough to give your nervous system
the encouragement it needs to make programming changes to
your operating system.

Rewards are a type of celebration, but they are not the most
important type. Microcelebrations, on the other hand, are
something that you could—and I'd even argue you should—
do every day. These celebrations are things like hugs, brags,
high fives, and plain old jumping up and down (either literally or figuratively). They are easily achievable and accessible
to you. They offer quick gratification—a nearly instant hit to
your nervous system. And they are typically free or low cost.
Rewarding yourself for small wins is one way to hack your

nervous system's programming. Remember back in chapter 6 we talked about the ways your nervous system might be operating on outdated programming? That programming was written for us as children but may no longer serve us. Rewarding your nervous system is one way to undo that programming. The goal is to offer your nervous system wins—through celebration—as you make progress so that it wants you to make more progress. In this way, you take your nervous system from barrier to breakthrough partner.

ACTION STEP:
BUILD A CELEBRATION MENU

Even if you feel like you haven't made any progress yet, I want you to stop and think about how you are going to celebrate. Decide what you are going to do—something accessible and immediate that will feel awesome to you—each time you have a win. Again, this is a pretty simple activity and yet so many people don't take the time to do it. The goal of this action step is to have a list of easy and immediately possible (don't need to be deferred) activities to pick from each time you have something to celebrate (which, if you do it right, could be on the daily). I even have clients who put this menu on small pieces of paper in a celebration jar and pick from the jar when it's time to throw a miniparty. To build out your celebration menu, consider the following prompts:

When I am happy, I enjoy . . .

When I want to pump myself up, I . . .

When I think about celebrating, I want to . . .

Give yourself permission to be creative and think big. There is no wrong answer.

Celebration, like so many things, is incredibly personal. First, like finishing, celebration doesn't have to be fancy. It can be as simple as sharing your success with a loved one or giving someone a joyful hug. It can also be quiet, like sitting and feeling appreciation or journaling about your win. Second, remember that microcelebrations are different than rewards. This isn't a list of things you will give or buy yourself when you've earned them. Microcelebration activities are things that you already have or are easy to do but that you will enjoy and appreciate. For example, I'm not getting a manicure every ten thousand words, but I am throwing a dance party when I hit a goal—I'm celebrating. That doesn't mean rewards are wrong—they have a place, too. But here, I'm talking about celebrating. If you are struggling to come up with a celebration menu, head to the resources section for a downloadable list to get you started.

Ultimately, the most important thing about developing this menu is using it. I suggest two triggers for a celebration:

1.   When you make any progress toward doing and having more of what matters to you, celebrate.
2.   When you do something that is contrary to one of your nervous system's old rules, celebrate. This one is important. When you act contrary to your programming, you want to show your nervous system not only that you didn't die (that you are

safe) but also that you are excited and happy about making a change.

If you've done all or even some of the action steps in the book up until this point, I celebrate you for doing the hard work to move in the direction of the happier, easier life you deserve. I want you to stop right now and throw yourself a miniparty. Pick one or two things off your celebration menu. Do them.

Finally, know that, while you can perhaps be too fancy, you can never celebrate too much. If you are struggling to move forward and all you do on a given Tuesday is take one microstep toward your destination, throw that microstep a microparty. The reality is our nervous system thrives on feeling good—on wins—so the more wins you can throw its way, the more it will be your partner as you move forward. Shocker: your nervous system likes to feel good. When you give your nervous system regular wins in the form of celebration, it seeks out more wins. So, give it a chance to feel good about what you've accomplished—no matter how seemingly small—and it is more likely to be on board to keep going.

On the hard days, remember that movement toward your destination, however small or imperfect, is progress. And on those days (and every day), throw that progress a party. Have some fun. Recognize that moving in the direction of what matters to you—moving in a priority-aligned way—is a gift to yourself and those around you, because it means you are putting your energy toward what has value to you. And when you choose to live that way, you will be happier.

Chapter 21

CHECKING YOUR ALIGNMENT

This chapter is for those currently thinking something like: *Now that I know where I want to go, I'm going to do all the things* right now! You know who you are: you start huge and burn out fast. You often end up overwhelmed by how much you have to do. If that's how you are approaching this, I'm going to ask you to *slow down.* I get it. In the past, slowing down has not served you. But I'm asking you to trust me when I tell you that if you want to live a more priority-aligned life, you might need to explore a different speed of operation.

This chapter is also for the rest of you—the ones who have started living in alignment with your priorities but are beginning to recognize that balancing your energy and priorities is an endless dance. One that requires continuous adjustment and editing, as well as slowing down and reevaluating when unhappiness or overwhelm starts to creep back in. If this hasn't happened to you yet, it will. I promise. A day will come when you realize that—like a car that has been driven over too many potholes—you are out of alignment. You will need to slow down, evaluate, and get yourself back into alignment.

There are two things to explore in this slowed-down state. On a macro level, make sure you are keeping the main thing the main thing. Be sure you are staying true to your priorities in the ways you spend your time and energy. On a micro level, keep the main thing the main thing on a weekly—and during particularly busy times, a daily—basis. Here's how.

You've taken the time to identify what really matters, what you value, and what is most important. Many people get that far but aren't thoughtful about putting that into practice on a continuous basis. It is really easy to fall back into attempting to do more to get more. If you are feeling pulled to do all the things, stop and go back to how you ranked this season's priorities. Really, go back to it. Read it. And then sit with it. If you didn't do that work, you may be experiencing the mounting tension created by failing to authentically name and claim what matters to you. Go back to chapter 16 now and order your priorities. Once you refocus on your priorities, return to all the things you were going to do and determine whether they support your identified priorities. Or have you chosen things you know you can get done because you want to feel accomplished? If you are used to measuring your productivity by to-dos checked off, I am asking you to make a change. The relevant question is no longer "How much did I get done?" It is "How am I feeling about what I've accomplished?" If you have thrown your energy around and checked off a bunch of meaningless boxes, you are no closer to happy than when you started. Repeat this review of your top priorities as often as necessary, even daily if need be.

As a general rule, here's how to continue to live in alignment with your priorities: make your priorities public, allocate resources to your priorities first, and when faced with a choice, choose what matters most. It will serve no one if you keep your priorities a secret. You will still feel the detrimental effects of the Authenticity Gap, and you won't be free to truly spend your time and energy on what matters most to you. I understand that it might feel scary to share your priorities with people whose opinions are important to you. I've lived through both sides of this and know the feelings intimately. I can tell you that honesty is almost always a gift. The people in your life who really care about you want you to be happy. And they also want to know what will make you happy, so they can help you to achieve it. That doesn't mean they won't have opinions or feelings on the matter, or that the conversation won't be difficult. However, on the other side of that conversation is freedom—the ability to live openly in a way that maximizes your happiness.

ACTION STEP:
PRIORITY PR

Consider who in your life needs to know about your priorities. Who might be impacted when you start to live in alignment with what matters to you rather than what matters to anyone else? This might include obvious people like your partner, your family, or your employer. It may also include less obvious people, like your coworkers or service providers. As with every exercise in this book, there is no right or wrong answer. In addition, you don't need to operate under any specific timeline. Simply recognize that to close your Authenticity Gap and your Physical Energy Gap, you will probably need to tell the people who will be impacted by what you are up to.

Step One: Who needs to know about your priorities?

If you are shifting your focus to your priorities, consider who will be impacted. Who will have less of your time and energy than they have been getting, and who will have more? Who will hear "no" more often and who will hear "yes"? Without worrying how the conversation will go, simply identify the who.

Step Two: Identify resistance.

You may have already communicated with some of the people you identified in step one—it's easy to have easy conversations. There will, however, be people with whom you have not talked about this. Identify those people and then consider:

What is holding you back from telling them?

Use the exercises in chapter 11 to work through those emotions so you can have the conversation.

Some of these conversations may be difficult or uncomfortable. Remember that your purpose in publicizing your priority isn't to convince someone that your most important thing is *the* most important thing. It is simply about letting them know what matters most to your happiness—there's no room for someone else's wrong or right in that equation. Once you've publicized your priorities, it will be easier to make the choices you need to spend your time and resources on what matters to you.

Now it's time to consider how you are matching resources to your priorities. Ordinarily, people plan their schedules around the things that "need" doing, without any consideration of the relative importance of those things. Then they try to use the leftover time to make progress on the things that actually matter. Sound backward? Because it is. It's like trying to drive to your destination in reverse—possible, but awkward, frustrating, and not very efficient.

Allocating resources to your priorities first can be difficult, especially if you are already busy and overwhelmed. If you can manage it, however, I highly recommend starting with a blank state and rebuilding your schedule and resource expenditure to match your priorities. If you want to do some radical editing, take a look at your schedule and to-do list for the next month and cross off everything that doesn't support your top priority— and perhaps the next two to three areas of focus if you have additional space. This approach is pretty aggressive, so it's not for everyone. If starting with a clean slate is too much, try the more conservative activity below to begin making room in your schedule to apply this forward-driving approach to future planning. I use this activity on a weekly, and sometimes daily, basis to make sure I'm living in alignment with my priorities.

ACTION STEP:
SUBTRACT SUNDAY

You can use this tool to evaluate how you want to spend your time—daily, weekly, or monthly.

Step One: Review your schedule and task list.

Look at your schedule and task list for the relevant time period. I like to do this weekly on Sundays (hence the name), but you can do it any day and for a longer period of time. Ask yourself:

How are these items supporting the top three to five things I've declared are most important to me in this season?

If you can't come up with an answer or have to stretch to answer for any item on your calendar or list, circle it.

Step Two: Subtract.

Review those circled items. And then cross them off.

If you can't get rid of all of them, get rid of some of them. Your nervous system will try to stop you—it will tell you that you will hurt someone's feelings or let someone down. If you are struggling with this, revisit the activities in chapters 11 and 12 about dealing with difficult feelings and about guilt. Or, if you aren't up for doing that work, decide that you are going to cross these things off anyway and that you'll deal with the consequences. That's right, you can choose to act instead of processing your feelings. Sometimes it's what is needed.

Sometimes crossing things off requires more than an eraser. Sometimes it means a difficult conversation. Where that is the case, I try to have those conversations right away. Remember, the best no is clear, honest, quick, and kind.

Step Three: Handle the new space.

Congratulations! By removing those things from your list or calendar, you've just created space. Now, how are you going to fill it? You can fill it with new random tasks, with activities related to your top priority, or with nothing. What you do with the space is up to you, but before you decide, consider:

What can I use this space for that will have the greatest positive impact on my happiness?

I'd suggest you go with whatever answer comes up—even if that answer is do nothing. Doing nothing can be self-care; and self-care matters. In fact, doing nothing is actually doing something. You can't have uptime without downtime. So if the message you are getting from your intuition is that you need to take some time for self-care—listen and rest.

Finally, even with the most careful editing, you must make choices when conflict exists—when time, energy, or resources are demanded at the same point for two things. In those times, you have a ready-built decision-making tool in the form of your desires, ranked in priority order. Since you've worked hard to create that list, you can use it to decide between competing demands confidently and without much analysis. Simply pick the most import-ant thing. Pick the thing you already identified matters to you more than other things. Pick your top priority unapologetically—because you don't need to apologize for doing what matters most to you. If you find yourself repeatedly picking something other than the top priority, you either have an Authenticity Gap issue or your nervous system is getting in your way.

When I began working with Stefanie, she identified her top priority as finding a new job. After several sessions, she had made little progress on her job hunt. She routinely spent the evening time she had earmarked for job searching either watching Netflix or socializing with friends. I pointed out to Stefanie that although she said finding a new job was *the* most important thing in her life, she wasn't behaving like that was true. She agreed that she wasn't prioritizing it, but she felt confused because she was confident finding a job mattered most. In other words, it wasn't an Authenticity Gap issue—she was being honest about what she wanted. I asked her what else might be going on. After some discussion, she identified two potential issues. First, she had a very busy day job—as a result she was often tired when she got home and didn't have much energy for job searching. On those nights she'd choose Netflix. Second, she was afraid that she wouldn't be able to find a new job, and that fear made her hesitant to even start looking. When she came home and had energy, it was easier, and safer, to choose spending time with people who made her feel good about herself. On those nights she'd socialize.

Stefanie ultimately came up with two solutions. To solve the long-day problem, two mornings a week she would get up early and spend thirty to sixty minutes doing job-search activities. She wanted to spend her daily energy on the thing that mattered most to her—before her current job had a chance to deplete it. To solve the fear problem, she agreed to enlist her friends in her job search. On those evenings when she was feeling energetic, she'd call a friend and talk through the jobs she was considering and be reminded by someone who knew her skill set why any employer would be lucky to have her. The additional benefit of being more open with her friends about her priority was that they were soon bringing her potential job opportunities.

Living a priority-aligned life requires being willing to edit. It requires being willing to eliminate things that take our energy—physical, mental, emotional, and financial—but don't matter to us. Most of us tend to be highly skilled at addition. We add more and more to our schedule, contorting ourselves and our energy to get it all done. We do this because we believe more is better—the more we do, the more we will have, and the happier we will be. I hope you see this is not the recipe for your happiness. If you want to work on doing more of what matters, so that you can have more of what matters, you will need to get better at subtraction. You will need to use a muscle that you probably haven't trained. And because it is untrained, strengthening it will require practice. You will need to edit yourself regularly. You will need to check in and confirm that you are not falling back into the trap of aiming for quantity over quality. You will make mistakes. And now you have a tool to check in and to correct those out-of-balance moments when they arise. And when you correct those moments, you will have yet another reason to celebrate.

Chapter 22

MEASURING SUCCESS

Remember, your happiness recipe is unique to you. What matters to you, and how you prioritize those things, is your decision alone. It follows then, that the only person's measurement of happiness or success that matters should be yours. In other words, you need to be your own ruler. You must evaluate your success against the measures you set for yourself, not against what society, your friends, or family tell you that you should achieve. This doesn't come naturally to many. Society tells us over and over in subtle and explicit ways that we need to have this phone, this car, this kind of house, this kind of body, this kind of hair, or this kind of job in order to be truly successful (and therefore happy). That's simply not true. And it's time to embrace your own unique blend of happiness.

In second grade I was a knock-kneed towhead with crooked teeth and probably crooked bangs. I was often just a little bit disheveled—one knee sock falling down or my shirt buttoned out of order. I was an only child with two working parents, so

I spent most of my free time at home by myself. I could usually be found roller-skating to "Eye of the Tiger" on our back deck, with my nose in a book, or making up games and songs. I had a rich imagination and absolutely no concern about sharing my inner world with the outer world. I didn't care what other people thought about me; I didn't know I was supposed to.

Then came third grade. In third grade, I attended a small parochial school—with two grades to a classroom. I had a wonderful third-grade teacher who was also a skilled woodworker. Each week, one student in the third or fourth grade would be selected to receive a carved word of the week. I waited and waited and waited for my turn. Other people got awesome words like *spectacular, amazing,* and *quick.* Every Friday, we'd rush in from recess and gather around the bulletin board humming with anticipation to see who'd get the word of the week. Finally, one sunny spring Friday, we came in and it was my turn. I was so excited . . . until I saw the word. The word, cut from wood and resting on thumbtacks over the certificate with my name, was *unique.* Literally, my word was *unique.*

My third-grade brain stuttered. I wasn't even sure what that word meant. Was it a good word? I asked the friend standing next to me to explain the word, then I asked another friend, and finally, I asked my parents that night over dinner. The gist of the meaning that my third-grade self took away from those conversations was that *unique* meant I wasn't like anyone else; it meant I was different. I didn't want to be different. I just wanted to fit in. I was so disappointed. This wasn't the word I'd waited almost a whole school year for.

Merriam-Webster's Collegiate Dictionary defines *unique* as "being without a like or equal." For a long time, *unique* set the tone for what I thought I didn't want to be. I didn't want to stand out. I didn't want to be special or different. I just wanted to be like everyone else. I didn't want my label to be *unique.* Fast-forward thirty-five-plus years, and I am finally at peace with being unique—with being without a like or equal. It is not a problem that I don't always think like everyone else—in fact, it's often a gift. It isn't a problem that I don't fit in with every group. I am comfortable being me. And in celebrating my uniqueness and embracing who I really am, I am finally free to be the best version of myself. Because, you see, if I am without equal, there is no one to measure myself against—I can only be my own ruler.

To truly live a priority-aligned life, you need to let go of comparison. No really. Priority-aligned living is completely individual. Nobody out there is living your life, and nobody out there shares your exact recipe for happiness. And so, to compare yourself to how another is spending their time as a measure of your success is always to compare apples to oranges. There is no comparison. Also, particularly in the age of social media, it's likely you are only seeing select parts of another person's situation. You are often comparing the inside of your life to only the outside of someone else's. In other words, you are comparing your whole self to only the shiniest and best parts of them—and that's no comparison at all. Your answers, your priorities, and your happiness are yours alone.

It would have been easy as I transitioned from a practicing attorney to law firm administration to compare where I was to where some of my close peers—with similar credentials— were at the same time. I could have looked at my good friend who had recently made partner at a large litigation law firm or the friend who was now my boss and wondered why I hadn't achieved what they had. I'd be flat-out lying if I said I never engaged in this train of thought. But the truth is, while they had achieved certain things I hadn't (like professional top-of-the-pyramid status), I also had things they didn't (like time and flexibility). And ultimately, the things I had were more important to me during that chapter of my life than the things they had. I'm not better than them, of course. I've watched these two wonderful women navigate their evolving seasons and make choices based on what was most important to them. And I'm grateful that, instead of comparing apples to oranges, we all celebrate how we are living in alignment with our priorities in each season.

ACTION STEP:
YOUR RULER

While you aren't setting goals (unless you want to), it is still important to think about how you will measure success in this season. You've got a list of things you want to accomplish; now is the time to figure out how you will know you are accomplishing them. For your top priority and each of the rest of your top three to five areas of focus, consider the following questions:

How will I know when I am successful?

How can I measure my progress in this area?

How will it feel when I'm successful?

Really consider how you (not anyone else) will know whether you are successful in this area. This might be measured in ultimate achievement or in progress. What matters is how you define success. For some categories, this will be easy. For example, if your top priority is positioning yourself to secure a promotion at work, you will know you are successful when you get the promotion. That said, it might be more difficult to measure incremental progress toward this destination.

By contrast, if your top priority is to have more time freedom, the measure of success will be more personal. Measuring progress might be achieved by looking at how many times in a given period you were able to travel or how much time you spent on self-care. Measuring ultimate success, however, may be more nebulous. That is not a problem. What is important is to have some measurement tool to check whether you are living in alignment with your priorities.

Finally, the last question may be the most important. Knowing how it will feel—and beginning to feel that feeling—will really allow you to draw yourself toward the outcome you want. In addition, if you find yourself describing a successful outcome you don't think will feel amazing, consider if that's really the outcome for you.

Ultimately, in living a priority-aligned life, what matters is what matters to you. This approach to living is not focused on what your friends or extended family think are markers of success. This approach is not focused on living up to your childhood ideal of success—unless that is still what you want. When you are living a priority-aligned life, your success will not be measured by anyone else's yardstick. You will be your own ruler.

Parting Thoughts

Before I was a lawyer, I went to college convinced I wanted to go to medical school. I had been dreaming about it for most of my life. Starting in sixth grade, I counted the years until I could do my residency. That year, I even wrote a research paper on a medical procedure called pneumothorax—complete with anatomical diagrams—and read medical dramas on the regular. I graduated from high school and headed off to college registered for a full slate of premed classes, with plans to rock them and then head straight to medical school—ideally at an Ivy League. Then, in my first year of college, I was met with an unprecedented level of freedom. At age seventeen, I was several thousand miles from home with seemingly no adult supervision. Nobody was making sure I went to class, did my homework, or ate something other than cereal for three meals a day.

The side effect of this drastic change was that I watched *Days of Our Lives* more regularly than I attended class—attending less than 50 percent of my first semester classes. (Sorry, Mom and Dad, I now recognize this was not very respectful of the resources you spent to put me on that campus.) I also ate a lot of Lucky Charms, slept excessively, and socialized like it was my job. All the classes I would need to prepare me for medical school weren't engaging to me. I certainly wasn't going to earn admission to an Ivy League medical school with the Bs and Cs I was getting at the end of my first semester—the first Bs and Cs of my life. I recognize that many amazing medical professionals don't go to Ivy League medical schools. But at that time in my life, under the cloud of a lot of shoulds, I thought that was the only possible path for me. Pretty quickly I decided medical school was out.

I wasn't sure what would be next. The only classes I found remotely interesting were my literature class and my political science classes. And that was probably because I could read, research, and write with ease—skills I'd learned in four years of high-quality high school debate. Ultimately, I fumbled my way through four years of college taking courses that played to my strengths and were a little bit off the beaten path. Soon graduation was looming, and I was still at loose ends. I was heading into the future with a decent GPA, a major in political science, and a minor in economics. But I didn't know what I was supposed to do, where I was supposed to go, or who I was supposed to be.

If I could go back to the spring of 1997, knowing what I know today, here's what I would tell my younger self. (Perhaps you need to hear some of this too.)

> The only thing you are supposed to do and be is you. And you are okay. You will be okay. It's not a big deal that you've shifted gears and are questioning what you thought you wanted to do, even though you thought it for a long time. It doesn't really matter what anyone else tells you about this shift—the only opinion that matters is your own. All you are supposed to

be is yourself—nothing more, nothing less. You have permission to figure out what will make you happy as you go. You have permission to choose to prioritize those things over what everyone else says and thinks you should do. This will be hard to do sometimes; but just because it is hard, doesn't mean it is wrong. Embrace your intuition. Listen to what your feelings—great and small—tell you about where your happiness lives.

Happiness is not a contest. It's not an achievement or an end state. Happiness, like balance, is a skill you practice. Your recipe for happiness can—and likely will—be different in every season of your life. This is just the beginning of a new season. A new season where you can decide what matters to you and what you need to be happy. A new season where you get to declare your priorities and where you can allow that declaration to govern how you spend your time and energy. A new season in a long series of seasons. A new season that will not— alone—define you, your worth, your success, or your legacy.

Take a little time now to recognize your season and think about what you want to have, where you want to go. Then consider what is standing between you and that destination—your behaviors, your feelings, your beliefs, your guilt, and your fear. Think about what those feelings are trying to tell you, listen to them, thank them, and then release them. Explore those beliefs and recognize that you have the power to change and overcome them. See that fear as a sign you are not staying still—you are moving and growing, and that is a good thing. Finally, remember this season is yours, this life is yours, and happiness is yours for the taking. All you need is your

1. authenticity—an honest understanding of what
    you really want, think, and feel right now, of what
    is most important to you;
2. aligned emotional energy—the beliefs and feel-
    ings that will support you as you go; and
3. aligned physical energy—action that matches
    what matters most to you.

Mix these things liberally and sprinkle them with celebration and fun. Then you can measure your success not just in
hours at the office, titles on a business card, or dollars in a bank
account, but by a life joyfully lived. You can live a happy, easier,
priority-aligned life right now. All you have to do is start.

ACKNOWLEDGMENTS

I sometimes describe myself as a collector of souls. I need to take a moment to express my deep appreciation for the souls who were instrumental in making this book a reality:

My husband, Don. His love and support on this project—and in life—has been foundational to my success.

My children, Hayley and Grant, who were willing to endure endless hours of discussion about how to write certain topics in this book and hours of me being sequestered, writing. I appreciate their patience, fresh perspective, and intelligence more every single day.

My parents, who were the best life guides I could have ever asked for. I've learned so much from watching them live priority-aligned lives focused on what truly matters to them.

My editor Jaime Fleres—who made me feel so supported in sending my book baby off into the world. Her input and touch have made this book markedly better.

My writing group—Anne, Becca, Ernesto, Katy, and Reija (and our fearless leader Alice)—they are some of the most recent additions to my collection of beautiful souls. They have grounded me, lifted me, encouraged me, taught me, and led me. I would not be here without them.

My friends and extended family, most especially Colleen, the first person I let see this book, but also all those who were willing to read and give feedback as the book developed—you know who you are. I appreciate your time, your care, and your support.

My coaching community—I am fortunate to know some of the most skilled and talented coaches ever. I am grateful for the friendship, connection, and support I've found there.

My readers—I am glad you are here. I am proud of you for wanting to grow and change, and I am hopeful that I've been able to be a part of that.

RESOURCES

Companion materials for this book can be found at
www.untanglehappiness.com/happinessrecipe.

Connect with Becky

- www.untanglehappiness.com
- On Instagram: the.butterfly.society
- On LinkedIn: www.linkedin.com/in/
  beckymorrisonbfs

Further reading

- Clear, James. *Atomic Habits: An Easy & Proven
  Way to Build Good Habits & Break Bad Ones.*
  New York: Avery, 2018.
- Dweck, Carol S. Mindset: *The New Psychology of
  Success.* New York: Ballantine Books, 2016.
- Hendricks, Gay. *The Big Leap: Conquer Your
  Hidden Fear and Take Life to the Next Level.* New
  York: HarperOne, 2010.
- McKeown, Greg. *Essentialism: The Disciplined
  Pursuit of Less.* New York: Crown Business, 2014.

- Porges, Stephen W. *The Pocket Guide to the Polyvagal Theory: The Transformative Power of Feeling Safe.* New York: W. W. Norton, 2017.
- Sinek, Simon. *Start with Why: How Great Leaders Inspire Everyone to Take Action.* London: Penguin Group, 2009.
- Van der Kolk, Bessel. *The Body Keeps the Score: Brain, Mind, and Body in the Healing of Trauma.* New York: Penguin Books, 2015.

ABOUT THE AUTHOR

 Rebecca C. Morrison is a mom, wife, and lawyer turned happiness coach. A graduate of Wellesley College and Georgetown Law, she also received an executive coaching certification from UC Berkeley. Rebecca worked in finance and Big Law for over twenty years before starting a business doing what she loves: helping other people become happier and more successful.

Rebecca spends her days helping clients uncover their own happiness recipe by applying the principles of priority-aligned living. Having shared these tools with people both informally and formally over the past two decades, she is thrilled to be sharing them with the world in her first book, *The Happiness Recipe*.

CPSIA information can be obtained
at www.ICGtesting.com
Printed in the USA
LVHW091654071221
705517LV00006B/321